TREASURES OF
THE HOOD MUSEUM OF ART
DARTMOUTH COLLEGE

HUDSON HILLS PRESS, NEW YORK
IN ASSOCIATION WITH
THE HOOD MUSEUM OF ART,
DARTMOUTH COLLEGE

Jacquelynn Baas
Hazel Anne Burrows
Malcolm Cochran
Phylis Floyd
Jeffrey L. Horrell
Barbara J. MacAdam
Tamara Northern
Lisa P. Quirk

WITH AN ESSAY BY
Charles W. Moore

TREASURES OF
THE HOOD MUSEUM OF ART
DARTMOUTH COLLEGE

FIRST EDITION

© 1985 by the Trustees of Dartmouth College, Hanover, New Hampshire

All rights reserved under International and Pan-American Copyright Conventions.

Editor and Publisher: Paul Anbinder
Copy editor: E. B. Sanders
Designer: Betty Binns Graphics/Betty Binns and Karen Kowles
Composition: Trufont Typographers
Manufactured in Japan by Toppan Printing Company

This project has been supported by a grant from the National Endowment for the Arts

Photography for this publication was supported in part by a gift from the Friends of the Hopkins Center and Hood Museum of Art

Published in the United States by Hudson Hills Press, Inc., Suite 301, 220 Fifth Avenue, New York, NY 10001.

Distributed in the United States by Viking Penguin Inc.

Distributed in Canada by Irwin Publishing Inc.

Distributed in the United Kingdom, Eire, Europe, Israel, and the Middle East by Phaidon Press Limited.

Distributed in Japan by Yohan (Western Publications Distribution Agency).

Library of Congress Cataloguing-in-Publication Data
Hood Museum of Art.
Treasures of the Hood Museum of Art, Dartmouth College.
Bibliography: p.
Includes index.
1. Art—New Hampshire—Hanover—Catalogues.
2. Hood Museum of Art—Catalogues. I. Baas, Jacquelynn, 1948– . II. Moore, Charles Willard, 1925– . III. Title.
N575.A65 1985   708.142'3   85-14526

ISBN 0-933920-71-7 (alk. paper)

CONTENTS

FOREWORD

Treasures of the Hood Museum of Art commemorates the opening of Dartmouth's new art museum. This splendid facility was made possible by a bequest from Harvey P. Hood of the Dartmouth class of 1918 and by the generosity of the Hood family and other supporters of the arts at Dartmouth. The exciting architecture of the new museum, by Charles Moore and Chad Floyd of Centerbrook Architects, is in itself a testimony to a renewed institutional commitment to the arts.

The selection of works from the college's collection recorded in this book reflects the breadth and quality of the artistic traditions of Dartmouth College. From the gift in 1773 of the beautiful commemorative monteith that Governor John Wentworth commissioned in honor of our first commencement of 1771, to the coming of the set of Assyrian reliefs in the mid-nineteenth century, to the execution in the 1930s of the world-famous mural cycle painted in Baker Library by José Clemente Orozco, and on to the present time, the history of art acquisitions at Dartmouth has been truly extraordinary. But over the years the college's extensive holdings have not been widely known.

Traditionally, college portraits have been on view in the library. In recent years, portions of the Dartmouth collection have been exhibited within the third-floor galleries of Carpenter Hall, the home of the Art History Department, and, since 1962, in Hopkins Center, where the Visual Studies Department holds its classes. Displays of ethnographic objects were for some years shown in Wilson Hall, while that structure housed our Anthropology Department. The opening of the Hood Museum of Art in the fall of 1985 not only honors and extends Dartmouth's past achievements of collecting and cherishing within the realm of the visual arts, it clearly marks an important new phase in the life of this institution.

Upon its conception in 1978, the Hood Museum was designated as a "laboratory for the study of works of art, from painting and sculpture to graphics and film; and man's artifacts, including a full spectrum of primitive and prehistoric cultures." Within such a context the potential of art to defy the customary boundaries of human culture and learning can now be fully explored on the Hanover Plain.

No less important, particularly for a college museum, is the delight that accompanies the perception of works of art, an experience that is educationally significant. We enjoy art not only for its intrinsic beauty, but also because we are curious. To understand a successful work of art—a genuine product of the human imagination—is also to discover something about who we are and what our place is on this earth. This is central to the ultimate goal of a liberal education.

DAVID T. McLAUGHLIN
President, Dartmouth College

PREFACE

ON the occasion of the dedication of the new Hood Museum of Art at Dartmouth College, it seems appropriate to showcase the Dartmouth collection. This book is intended to provide an informative overview, faithful to the quality and scope of the collection. The guiding principle has been to offer a representative selection of works of the highest quality. Decisions about which objects to include have not been easy, and in the process of trimming our list of candidates, we have learned much about the variety and distinction of the objects Dartmouth has collected over a period of more than two centuries. We hope that this volume will convey something of our excitement at seeing them gathered together for the first time in one place.

In addition to information about each work, this book also includes a general history of the museum collections at Dartmouth, essays on the development of different areas of the art collection, and Charles Moore's account of the process of designing the new museum. In the future, we plan to publish catalogues that focus on specific aspects of the collection. As a handbook, *Treasures of the Hood Museum of Art* is selective rather than comprehensive. Its purpose is to awaken interest in the collection that these objects represent.

I would like to acknowledge those individuals whose efforts have made this book possible. Generous contributions of time and expertise were made by Maxwell Anderson, Kathleen Corrigan, Julie Jones, Jim Jordan, Jan Lancaster, Judith Lerner, Dr. Hartley Neal, Nathan Whitman, Matthew Wiencke, and Marshall Wu. Special mention is due Kenneth Cramer, Philip Cronenwett, and the staff of Special Collections, Dartmouth College Library, where a good deal of research was accomplished in a relatively short time. Jeffrey Horrell and the staff of the Sherman Art Library also deserve special thanks.

Churchill P. Lathrop was kind enough to read the manuscript and share with us his comments, and David Robbins provided valuable editorial assistance. We are exceedingly grateful to Charles W. Moore for taking time out from his busy schedule to contribute the essay "Planning the Hood Museum of Art."

I would like to extend warm thanks to the staff of the Hood Museum of Art, both those who contributed to this publication as authors and those who made the book possible in other, no less vital, ways. Phylis Floyd of the Hood staff guided the manuscript through press and should be particularly thanked. Our publisher, Paul Anbinder of Hudson Hills Press, deserves special mention for his enthusiasm and patience. Hudson Hills's editor, Elma Sanders, and designer, Betty Binns, each made valuable contributions to this book, and we are most grateful to them.

Final thanks must be given to the National Endowment for the Arts and to the Friends of the Hopkins Center and Hood Museum of Art for financial support of this publication. Without such enlightened patronage, neither this book nor the events that occasioned it would have been possible.

JACQUELYNN BAAS
Director, Hood Museum of Art

A HISTORY OF THE DARTMOUTH COLLEGE MUSEUM COLLECTIONS

BY JACQUELYNN BAAS

THE collections of art and artifacts at Dartmouth College can be traced back to the period of the school's founding by the Reverend Eleazar Wheelock in 1769. At the second commencement, in 1772, Dr. John Phillips gave the young college £175 with which to acquire a "philosophical apparatus." [1] On October 26 of the same year, the Reverend David McClure, a tutor at the college, wrote to President Wheelock, "I have collected a few curious Elephants Bones found about six hundred miles down the Ohio, for the young Museum of Dartmouth, which I shall forward to Philadelphia the first conveyance." [2] Dartmouth's art collection dates from March of 1773, when the college received a magnificent silver monteith from John Wentworth, royal governor of New Hampshire and trustee of the young institution. The monteith and portraits of Wheelock, Phillips, and Wentworth are reproduced in this volume (numbers 85–88).

The promise of a "philosophical apparatus" and "a few curious Elephants Bones" may seem an odd beginning for the collection that has evolved into the Hood Museum of Art two centuries later; however, Dartmouth's traditional role as an undergraduate college in the New England "wilderness" fostered a peculiar kind of museum history. In the earliest days of the college, its remote setting inspired an active commitment to providing students with classifiable examples of the "natural and moral world." During the tumultuous years of 1815 to 1820, the school's resources were drained by the Dartmouth College Case, a bitter fight to remain a private college rather than become a state university (see pages 13 and 102). This period and the years of slow recovery that followed hindered the development of Dartmouth's museum collections. Thereafter, with little expectation of graduate programs in the humanities or social sciences, the college allowed its collections of art and artifacts to be shifted about in response to teaching and display needs.

Dartmouth did not have a building for its art collection until Carpenter Hall was completed in 1929. The Butterfield Museum of Paleontology, Archaeology, Ethnology, and Kindred Sciences had been built in 1895–96, but it was torn down in 1928 to make way for Baker Library. At this time the "cream of the collections" [3] in the natural sciences was skimmed off by the various academic departments for use in teaching, while the ethnographic and remaining natural history items were transferred to the library's former home in Wilson Hall. From 1928 on, there was an increasing tendency to consider the Museum as an independent entity; thus the "Dartmouth College Museum," consisting of mainly ethnographic and natural history material, remained in Wilson until 1974. In that year the college made the decision to divest itself of its entire natural history collection and to merge the administration of its extensive ethnographic, archaeological, and historical collections with that of the art collection. In 1976 it was decided to seek funding for a centralized museum, a goal that became attainable in 1978 with a major bequest from Harvey P. Hood, Dartmouth class of 1918.

What is now known as the Hood Museum of Art is thus both one of the oldest and one of the youngest museums in America. It is also, as far as I know, the only college museum responsible for every object of historical and aesthetic value at its institution. With a collection of about 40,000 objects, a full-time staff of twelve, and a new building designed by the American architect Charles W. Moore, the Hood Museum has emerged as a vigorous participant in the life of Dartmouth College and in the museum world at large.

1772–1804
THE EARLY YEARS

The Reverend David McClure's reference to a "young Museum of Dartmouth" in his 1772 letter to President Wheelock would seem to be the earliest record of a college museum in America. [4] His comment may well have been meant rhetorically, however, with an eye to the future. McClure made no mention of a museum in his diary, although his entry for October 28–29, 1772, documents a circuitous shipment of artifacts for Dartmouth: "Forwarded to the care of our worthy friend, John Bayard Esq., of Philada., a Box to be forwarded to Boston, to the care of my friend Henry Knox, there; containing some Mammoth's bones, some skins (Buffaloes, &c.) seeds, human bones picked up on Braddock's field &c." McClure's diary also informs us of a visit on July 7, 1774, to Cambridge, Massachusetts, where he "lodged with Mr. J. Winthrop, the Librarian, & next day viewed the Library, Museum, & returned to Boston." [5] The museum collections at Harvard and at Yale, which was the alma mater of both Wheelock and McClure, would have provided the likeliest models for their own plans.

In the eighteenth century there was no concept of specialized museums as we think of them today. The term "museum" generally referred to a "philosophical apparatus" (a standard set of scientific equipment) and a "cabinet of curiosities," which might consist of anything from art objects to fossils, ethnographic artifacts, or souvenirs of important or strange events. American museum collections of this period reflected the assumption that every aspect of the world—including humankind in all its manifestations as well as natural phenomena—was to be studied with the aim of reaching a more perfect understanding of God and his creation. McClure's diary alerts us to the centrality of this attitude in Dartmouth's early years and to the consequent importance the college assigned to the natural sciences. In his remarks on prehistoric discoveries near the salt licks of Ohio, where he obtained the "Mammoth's bones" for Dartmouth, McClure strikes a typical note of scientific enthusiasm nourished by faith.

It has been conjectured that the Mammoth was carnivorous. I should imagine, however, that it found a more easy and abundant subsistence in the luxuriant produce of the earth, in wild fruits, grass, bushes and the succulent limbs of trees; not to notice the difficulty which so bulkey an animal would find to catch the small & agile game of the woods, and the ease with which they could keep out of the way.

This greatest of the works of the Creator, among the beasts that ever roamed over the earth, must have been, to judge from the bones already found, not less than 16 or 18 feet in heighth. [6]

Although this eighteenth-century passion for observing, collecting, and speculating, directed by what was still a

"New World" exhilaration, lacked the interest in systematic study that would develop later in the nineteenth century, Native American artifacts were a standard component of the "cabinet" of the period. The concern for ethnographic authenticity that inspired these early collections is reflected in a 1768 letter from Dartmouth's founder, Eleazar Wheelock, to the college's patron, the earl of Dartmouth.

May it please your Lordship, I herewith present you a small specimen of the produce and manufacture of the American wilderness. I have been sometime waiting to be able to offer your Lordship that, which is perfectly simple, and without the least mixture of any foreign merchandize; but our traders have penetrated so far into their country, that I have hitherto found that to be impracticable, unless I had taken some articles, which were defaced by use. The pipe I here present you, is covered with porcupine quills, the bowl is stone. The longer string or braid is that, which they bind their burdens with for their backs, the broad part of it in the middle goes over their heads, and is wrought with a moose's mane. The lesser string is such as they use to bind their captives with; and the substance of both is elm bark, which they manufacture something after the manner which we do flax. The tobacco pouch they hang upon the right shoulder, and under the left arm. The knife case hangs from their neck upon their breast. The brass, tin, and beads in the several articles, they now use instead of wampom, which they make of shells, horns, and houghs of animals; the coloring is with roots and barks—and all is manufactured with their fingers.[7]

Thanks to such enthusiasm, Dartmouth's extensive collection of Native American artifacts dates from the earliest period of the college.

Although John Phillips's 1772 gift of £175 for a philosophical apparatus augured well for the immediate development of a museum collection, the War of Independence cut the young college's lifeline to England. The funds had been entrusted to Governor Wentworth, who was asked by the trustees to obtain such an apparatus from "his Friends in England."[8] President Eleazar Wheelock died in April 1779. In August of that year, the trustees appointed a committee to "prepare triplicate letters to Governor Wentworth requesting information from him relative to the disposal of one hundred and seventy five pounds lawful money given by the honorable

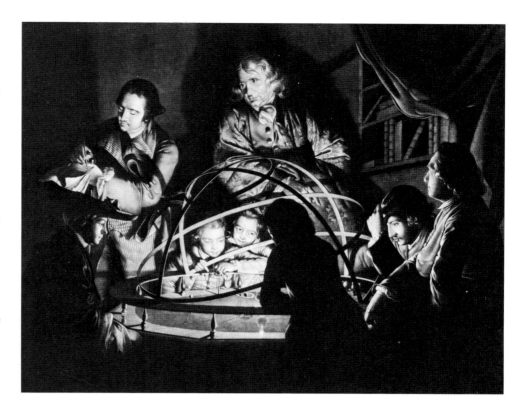

FIGURE 1   Joseph Wright of Derby (English, 1734–1797), *A Philosopher Giving a Lecture on the Orrery*. Mezzotint by William Pether (1731–1795) after the painting, published by John Boydell, 1768. Yale Center for British Art, Paul Mellon Collection.

John Phillips Esq. in the year 1772, for the purpose of procuring a philosophical apparatus for this college."[9]

Eleazar Wheelock was succeeded as president of Dartmouth College by his son, John Wheelock. Even before the formal end of the war in 1783, John Wheelock was authorized by the trustees to set forth for Europe "to solicit benefactions for this Institution."[10] Delayed by a British blockade of the Delaware River near Philadelphia in November of 1782, Wheelock and his youngest brother, James, finally sailed from Boston on January 3, 1783. The brothers seem to have been moderately successful in their fund-raising efforts on the Continent, and in July they were among the first Americans to visit England after the cessation of hostilities. Although Wheelock does not appear to have succeeded in raising immediate operating funds for the college there, he did make acquisitions for the library and museum.

While in England, as on the continent, [he] procured some coins and articles appreciated by the *virtuosi*. By the benevolence of Paul Wentworth, esq. [cousin of the former governor], Doctor Rose, and other friends to the college, some valuable philosophical instruments were obtained, and others promised, the making of which the two former kindly

engaged to superintend, and forward the whole, so soon as completed, to America. A way, besides, was preparing to provide natural curiosities for a museum. Those instruments, with their additions, well constructed, forming an apparatus sufficient for all the more important experiments and observations in Natural Philosophy, afterwards arrived [James and one of the president's other brothers, Eleazar, fetched them in 1785]; and at the same time a curious and valuable collection of stones and fossils from India, and different parts of Europe, for the museum, from the beneficent Mr. Forsythe, keeper of the king's gardens, at Kensington.[11]

The long-sought philosophical apparatus consisted of an "air pump, orrery, standing telescope with achromatic lenses, an elegant set of the mechanical powers, thermometer and a barometer."[12] The orrery, or "cosmoscope," was a mechanical device that illustrated the movements of the solar system. The excitement attending the use of these scientific instruments of the Enlightenment is conveyed by a contemporary work by the English artist Joseph Wright of Derby, *A Philosopher Giving a Lecture on the Orrery* (fig. 1).

A front View of DARTMOUTH COLLEGE, *with the* CHAPEL *&* HALL.

FIGURE 2 *Dartmouth Hall*, engraving by Samuel Hill after a drawing by J. Dunham, published 1793.

Since the apparatus was finally obtained through the generosity of the college's friends in England, the Phillips donation (which Governor Wentworth had safely deposited in a London bank) was available for other European purchases. John Wheelock reported to the trustees on April 20, 1784, that in light of the impending gift Dr. Phillips had "expressed his willingness that [his donation] be applied to the procuring of books for the library."[13]

As with other American colleges founded before the nineteenth century, the history of Dartmouth's museum collections is intertwined with that of its library. Until 1791 the philosophical apparatus, natural history specimens, and other "curiosities" probably were housed along with parts of the library collection in the first College Hall, finished in 1771.[14] (Prior to 1785 some objects may have been kept in Bezaleel Woodward's house, along with the library books.) In 1790 the board of trustees voted to install the apparatus above the library in the middle room on the third floor of Dartmouth Hall, which would be completed in the fall of 1791 (fig. 2).[15] Both the museum and the library were placed under the care of Bezaleel Woodward, professor of mathematics and philosophy and one of the two permanent members of the faculty at that time.[16]

Nothing better clarifies the pedagogical, ancillary role of the early museum collection than a trustee committee report of August 25, 1795, proposing an annual apportionment "for the respective offices of Secretary, Treasurer & Librarian, & for care of the Museum & Apparatus." The committee agreed that "the care of the Museum & Apparatus ought to be considered as belonging to & being a part of the duty of the Professor of Mathematicks & natural Philosophy & is to be considered in this point of view in the grant of salary to the one in that office." The librarian, on the other hand, was to "receive one fourth of the payments for the use of the Library, the board [of trustees] being at the expenses of an assistant."[17] Thus, while the library was accorded an independent role, with the librarian's salary tied to the use of its collection, the museum was defined as part of the regular curricular program and placed under faculty control.

The collection of paintings at Dartmouth College originated in 1793 with the commission of a portrait of Dr. John Phillips (number 86) on the occasion of his retirement as a trustee. At the same time, the trustees commissioned a posthumous portrait of the founder of the college, Eleazar Wheelock (number 85). Both works were completed and delivered in 1796. The development of the college's portrait collection is discussed

below (page 102) in the introduction to the section on American art. It is worth noting, however, that the college commissioned Joseph Steward, an alumnus of the class of 1780, to execute the portraits of Phillips and Wheelock. In addition to painting, Steward maintained a private museum in his studios at Hartford, Connecticut, after the fashion of his famous contemporary, Charles Willson Peale, whose privately owned and operated museum in Philadelphia opened in 1786. In his diary entry for August 31, 1772, David McClure reported finding a human skull and jawbone on Braddock's field, "which I afterwards presented to Mr. Stewart's [sic] Museum in Hartford."[18] These were probably some of the same items that were originally sent back to Dartmouth (see the diary entry for October 1772, quoted at the outset of this essay). It seems likely that the vigorous early growth of Dartmouth's museum collection owed much to the shared interests of these men.

Unlike the "museum" collection, the college portraits remained the responsibility of the librarian of the college well into the twentieth century. Many of the college's finest portraits are still on view in Baker Memorial Library. The presence there of the portraits and the important mural by José Clemente Orozco (discussed below) makes Baker Library an essential stop on any art tour of the campus.

On September 7, 1796, the following account appeared in both the Worcester *Massachusetts Spy* and the Boston *Columbian Centinel*:

Elias Hasket Derby, Esq. of Salem, has lately made a liberal donation to the Museum of Dartmouth College. Among other valuable and rare curiosities he has presented the Zebra, an African animal, a valuable acquisition to the curious in natural history; besides many other rarities from Asia and the Northwest coast of America. It is a happy circumstance that commerce may become the road to philosophy, as well as to wealth; and that those who are increasing the respectability of this country by enlarging its commercial interest, have inclination and taste to increase the interest of science at home.

Mr. Derby's stuffed zebra was destined to become part of Dartmouth lore. In his 1932 *History of Dartmouth College*, L. B. Richardson notes that the zebra, "unlike a properly regulated museum piece, was in the habit of appearing in incongruous places, such as the roof of the chapel or the belfry of the 'College' [Dartmouth Hall], thus requiring laborious transportation back to its normal abode." [19] In 1798 a serious fire broke out in Dartmouth Hall. John King Lord's 1916 *History of Dartmouth College* contains an amusing account of the priorities dramatized by the rescue of the college's collections.

The different phases of anxiety exhibited by members of the Faculty amused the students so much that reminiscences of it were handed down by tradition almost to the present day. All, of course, rushed breathless to the scene. Professor Smith was calling out to save the library, while Professor Woodward pleaded for the air pump, and the President [John Wheelock] at the same time shouted to save the zebra. [20]

The 1798 fire seems indeed to have resulted in some damage to the museum collection. The Trustees' Records for August 22, 1798, report a vote that "Mr. Ranna Cossit [a senior at the college] be allowed the sum of twenty-four dollars for his time in attending to repairs and arrangements of the Museum and apparatus the year past."

On August 27 Professor Woodward "requested to be excused from further care of the Museum." Although he continued nominally to supervise the collection, the daily tasks were officially passed on to a succession of tutors and graduates. On August 26, 1802, the trustees established what amounted to a one-year postgraduate position called "Inspector of the Museum." The appointee was paid ten dollars annually and charged to "admit company into

the Museum two hours each week in term time and also on public days," but was "under no obligation to admit company at any other time." [21]

1804–1828
NEGLECT OF THE COLLECTIONS,
AN ATTACK ON THE MUSEUM,
AND THE DARTMOUTH COLLEGE CASE

In 1804 Bezaleel Woodward died. John Hubbard assumed the post of professor of mathematics and philosophy and thus also the supervision of the museum. According to John King Lord, Hubbard was "a man of gentle temper, pleasing manners and scholarly taste," but the museum collection suffered from his neglect of official responsibilities.

After the death of Professor Woodward the philosophical department rather declined. His successor [Hubbard] being much devoted to music gave less attention to the care of the apparatus than could have been desired. Professor Adams coming to the office on the death of Professor Hubbard in 1810 found the apparatus greatly out of repair and of little value. It was much scattered about and some of it was lost. . . . We have no record of any other additions made during this period of depression. [22]

An even greater misfortune befell the museum collection in 1811. At this time, Dartmouth Hall was so arranged that student rooms on the upper floors of the north wing and the south wing were connected by a corridor on the first floor; students had to travel several flights of stairs to visit friends in the opposite wing. On the second floor, access between the two wings was blocked by the library; on the third floor, by the room housing the museum. According to a student account published several generations later, "this arrangement was very distasteful to the students, some of whom, in 1811, testified as much by blowing down the walls of the museum with a cannon, thereby nearly wrecking the whole building." [23]

We might today view this assault as a revolutionary call for user-responsive architecture. Nevertheless, the damage to the building and to the museum collection cannot have been negligible. A surviving letter from James Bartlett (1792–1837) to his Dartmouth roommate, Asa Hazen, contains a hint that one object of the attack may have been the college's philosophical apparatus itself. On December 2, 1811, Bartlett wrote from Salisbury, New Hampshire:

Reports of the most terrible kind are circulating at this place, respecting the "Institution." It is said B. Pierce is expelled. Also Kittredge, Philbrick and others whose names I have not learn't. . . . Please to write the next mail and inform me all the circumstances. —what the cause of their expulsion—how many there were expelled and who they were, . . . the Philos [apparatus]—whether there have been any more attacks made upon it. etc. etc. [24]

For "B. Pierce," at least, the cannon incident seems to have launched a brilliant career. Benjamin Kendrick Pierce, a senior law student and probably the leader of the group (Samuel Philbrick and Jonathan Kittredge were juniors), joined the army after his expulsion and earned an illustrious reputation during the Seminole War of 1835. Fort Pierce, Florida, was named after him. A biography published in the *Fort Pierce News-Tribune* contains this diplomatic synopsis of Pierce's early career: "When the War of 1812 started . . . he left college and obtained a commission as 1st lieutenant in the 3rd artillery regiment, probably on the basis of his earlier training in his father's militia." [25]

The fate of the museum immediately following the 1811 cannon attack is unclear. Lord says that "between 1812 and 1819 nearly $1,000 was expended for a new apparatus," albeit one of inferior quality. [26] The Dartmouth College treasurer's reports for the years immediately following the attack show that Inspectors of the Museum continued to be paid $10 per year. The tensions that would lead to the Dartmouth College Case were already building, however, and there can be little doubt that the growing schism between President John Wheelock and the college trustees during the years 1810 to 1815 had as disruptive an effect on the museum's development as on the rest of the college. In the famous Dartmouth College Case, the position of the trustees was defended against that of the State of New Hampshire by the nation's foremost orator, Daniel Webster, of the class of 1801. The result was a Supreme Court decision for the college in February 1819, reaffirming its status as a private institution. Financially, however, it was a full decade before Dartmouth recovered its strength.

FIGURE 3 **Ammi Burnham Young** (1798–1874), architect, *Presentation Drawing for Wentworth and Thornton Halls* (Wentworth to the left of Dartmouth Hall, Thornton to the right), about 1828.

FIGURE 4 **Sylvanus J. F. Thayer** (1842–1893), architect, *Presentation Drawing for the Dartmouth College Library* (Wilson Hall), about 1884. Hood Museum of Art, transfer from Facilities Planning, D.983.50.

1828–1928
NEW BUILDING PROGRAMS AND MIGRATIONS OF THE COLLECTIONS

By the time President Nathan Lord arrived on the Dartmouth scene in October of 1828, the college was entering a new period of growth. Thornton and Wentworth Halls, on either side of Dartmouth Hall, were nearing completion (fig. 3). Thornton Hall was the new home not only of the Dartmouth College Library, but of a Dartmouth Gallery of Paintings as well.[27] The paintings would accompany the library on each of its moves—to Thornton in the late 1820s, to Reed in 1840, to Wilson in 1885, and, in the case of the portraits, to Baker in 1928. The "museum" collection, however, comprising scientific, ethnographic, archaeological, and natural history objects, remained in Dartmouth Hall until the completion of Reed Hall in 1840, when they were reunited for

thirty years with the Gallery of Paintings and the library. Then they began a separate series of migrations—to Culver Hall (since demolished) in 1871, to Butterfield Hall (also demolished) in 1895, and finally to Wilson Hall in 1928.

Dartmouth's most important museum acquisition of the nineteenth century was its set of Assyrian reliefs (number 1), which reached Hanover late in 1856. In terms of quality, Dartmouth's six reliefs from the Northwest Palace of Ashurnasirpal II (883–859 B.C.) are probably the finest in the world after those in the British Museum. Dartmouth not only has more of these reliefs than any other college or university collection, it also possesses examples of all but one of the figural types contained in the palace.

The reliefs were obtained for the college by the Reverend Austin Hazen Wright, a member of the Dartmouth class of 1830 and a missionary in Persia, at the request of Professor Oliver Payson Hubbard. As professor of chemistry, mineralogy, and geology and librarian of the college, Professor Hubbard had charge of both the museum and the library. On February 17, 1853, Professor

Hubbard wrote Reverend Wright asking whether Wright might not be able to acquire for his alma mater "some mementoes of the ancient cities now opened on the Tigris," adding that "Williams College has, from some of her graduates, received some."[28]

In fact, there was a lively competition for these reliefs among American missionaries in the area. The archaeological discoveries along the Tigris, begun by the Englishman Austen Henry Layard in 1845, were widely regarded as proof of biblical history. This fact helps to explain the competition by American missionaries to obtain for their affiliated educational institutions examples of these impressive monuments to a heathen king. Of the approximately ninety-five reliefs from Ashurnasirpal's Northwest Palace that are today in the United States, fifty-four were acquired by American missionaries.

Fortunately for Dartmouth, Reverend Wright had good connections with Colonel Henry C. Rawlinson, who was in charge of British excavations in the area. In June 1854 Hubbard wrote to Wright that Mrs. Hubbard had recently seen some reliefs and letters at Yale that had been sent there by a "Rev. Mr. Williams." Hubbard warned Wright that Williams had referred in his letters to six slabs that Rawlinson was reserving for Dartmouth, and that Williams had stated, "It is possible that even a <u>king</u> may go to Dartmouth, but if it can be honorably got for Yale, I will get it." Wright got the "king." One of the other missionaries peevishly wrote at the time, "As Dartmouth had first choice, that college has a fine collection and little more than duplicates were left for us."[29] Sir Henry Rawlinson was awarded an honorary degree by the college in 1857.

When they first arrived at Dartmouth in 1856, the reliefs were installed in Reed Hall. Since then, portions of them have been displayed in various locations with either the art or the "museum" collections. At one point, half of them were on view with the "antiquities" in Wilson Hall, while the others were installed with the art collection in Carpenter Hall. Now, newly cleaned and reassembled thanks to the generosity of the Friends of the Hopkins Center and Hood Museum of Art and the National Endowment for the Arts, they form a focal point for the permanent collection of the Hood Museum.

On June 25, 1884, cornerstones were laid for both Rollins Chapel and the college library, Wilson Hall (fig. 4). Speaking for the trustees at the ceremony, the Reverend Alonzo H. Quint clarified that Wilson was also intended to be a home for the painting collection, but only temporarily.

The upper floor will be given at present to the fine collection of portraits and other paintings rapidly accumulating, for which so much is due to our graduate and Trustee, Benjamin F. Prescott, late Governor of the State. But we doubt not that, before long, some one will affix his name to an Art Gallery totally distinct, and placed somewhere in our picturesque grounds.

The cornerstone for Wilson Hall was laid by Benjamin Franklin Prescott, a member of the Dartmouth class of 1856 and an important influence in the development of the college's portrait collection. Like Quint, Prescott remarked on the double need met by Wilson.

In this distinguished presence I now place in position the cornerstone of Wilson Hall, which when completed, will be an ornament to this village, and will supply a want long felt by this institution as a place of safety to its works of art and its large and valuable library.[30]

The airy, skylit room on the second floor of Wilson Hall that housed the Dartmouth Gallery of Paintings (figs. 5a and b) today is part of the arts expansion program of Hopkins Center. Newly renovated, with its marvelous iron strutting left intact, it serves as a rehearsal space for the drama department.

FIGURES 5 a and b   Interior views of the Dartmouth Gallery of Paintings in Wilson Hall, late nineteenth century.

In 1892 Ralph W. Butterfield, Dartmouth class of 1839, left to the college the bulk of his estate for the purpose of "founding and forever maintaining a chair and professorship in paleontology, archaeology, ethnology and other kindred subjects; and for the erection of a building to cost not less than thirty thousand dollars, for the purpose of keeping, preserving and exhibiting specimens illustrating aforesaid branches."[31] The cornerstone for the central edifice of Butterfield Hall—the Butterfield Museum of Paleontology, Archaeology, Ethnology, and Kindred Sciences—was laid in 1895. After it was completed in 1896, Butterfield Hall (fig. 6) housed, in addition to the museum collection, the departments of zoology, botany, geology, sociology, psychology, and law.

Unfortunately, Butterfield's amateur interest in paleontology and the related fields of archaeology and ethnology did not correspond to the college's actual needs at the time, and the Butterfield Museum had a relatively brief existence. Badly sited, the building was torn down in 1928 to open a vista to a new, larger library, the Baker Memorial Library, which was dedicated at the commencement ceremony of that year. Parts of the museum collection were dispersed to their related departments to be used in teaching. The bulk of the material,

however, was transferred to the library's former home in Wilson Hall.

In retrospect, Ralph Butterfield seems to have been about fifty years ahead of his time. In 1946 Elmer Harp, Jr., would be appointed curator of anthropology in the College Museum, Wilson Hall, and in 1961 the anthropology faculty and staff would move into Wilson, thus creating the kind of teaching-museum operation that Butterfield had originally envisioned. This arrangement lasted for more than twenty years, a period during which the discipline of anthropology was broadened and diversified. In 1982 the department decided to relocate once again in order to make it possible for Wilson Hall to be a part of the building program of Hopkins Center and the new Hood Museum of Art. The anthropology department now resides in Carpenter Hall, and the ethnographic objects have been integrated into the collection of art and artifacts of the Hood Museum.

1929–1962
THE CARPENTER AND HOPKINS CENTER ART GALLERIES

The formal study of art at Dartmouth had its beginnings in the 1890s. George Dana Lord and Frank Gardner Moore taught classical art, while "modern" art (meaning art from the Renaissance to the nineteenth century) was taught by Arthur Sherburne Hardy, professor of

engineering. In 1905 Homer Eaton Keyes, Dartmouth class of 1900, was appointed assistant professor of modern art. Under his leadership a centralized art department was established on the top floor of the new, brick Dartmouth Hall (its wooden predecessor had burned to the ground in 1904), in the approximate location of the cannon attack on the museum a century earlier. In 1913 Keyes became business director of the college, and in 1921 he left Dartmouth to found and edit the highly successful art magazine *Antiques*, which he headed until his death in 1938.

Keyes was succeeded in the art department by George Breed Zug, who added to the curriculum the study of American painting, the graphic arts, and city planning—a radically modern curriculum for the time. Under Zug the department also organized special exhibitions, such as the first exhibition of work by members of the art colony at Cornish, New Hampshire, which was shown in the Little Theater of Robinson Hall in January 1916.

In 1921 the art department moved to larger quarters in Culver Hall, in space recently vacated by the chemistry department. Here, the collection of prints and photographs could expand, along with the art library. But this was a

temporary arrangement. In December 1927 Frank P. Carpenter of Manchester, New Hampshire, gave President Ernest Martin Hopkins funds to erect a building specifically for the art department. Carpenter Hall (fig. 7) was officially opened on June 14, 1929. Mildred Morse was the art curator, Dorothy Lathrop the exhibitions designer, and Maude French the art librarian. The *Guide to the Building and Special Exhibits* published on that occasion stated for the first time the "under one roof" theme that would become a leitmotif for subsequent art projects at Dartmouth.

Carpenter Hall provides a home for all the interests pertaining to the visual arts at Dartmouth. The building not only constitutes a complete teaching unit for the courses in Art and Archaeology, it also houses under one roof . . . a well-equipped Art Library, a central collection of photographs and lantern slides, a considerable collection of prints and colored reproductions, galleries for rotating exhibits of special and general interest, an up-to-date public lecture hall, well-lighted studios for the convenience of those who like to draw, paint, or model, and rooms for group discussions. . . . Consistent with the principles of an educational program which emphasizes the interrelation of all human interests, the building has been designed quite as much to serve the whole College as to provide suitably for the department of Art and Archaeology. Only those familiar with the inadequacy and scattered nature of such facilities as have been hitherto available can appreciate the importance of this splendid addition to the equipment of the College.

In order to make it possible for the exhibition rooms to have skylights, the galleries were placed on the third floor of the building. In retrospect, it may have been this decision that prevented eventual expansion of the Carpenter galleries into a full-fledged art museum. Out of the way of normal student traffic, these elegant galleries (fig. 8) never completely fulfilled their potential. But the art department had further plans for bringing art into the lives of the students. The Carpenter Hall *Guide* concludes, "Although no regular courses of instruction in the practice of drawing and painting are offered at present, facilities are provided for students who wish to pursue these interests as an extracurricular activity. From time to time advice and criticism may be received from visiting professionals." This modest statement was a harbinger of Dartmouth's distinguished artist-in-residence program.

Carpenter Hall was completed in 1929, just before the Great Depression. It was not long, however, before the chairman of the art department, Artemas Packard, along with Churchill P. Lathrop, who had joined the department in the fall of 1928, were plotting to

obtain the services of one of the great Mexican muralists to decorate their new building and provide students with a vivid example of work done in the revived Renaissance technique of fresco painting. Packard and Lathrop smoothed the way for their idea by installing Dartmouth's first artist-in-residence in the art studios on the top floor of Carpenter: Carlos Sanchez, Dartmouth class of 1923. Lathrop and Packard also used the Carpenter galleries to hold several exhibitions of drawings and prints by José Clemente Orozco, the muralist they favored for Dartmouth.

Through the generosity of John D. Rockefeller, Jr., and the enthusiasm of his wife, Abby Aldrich Rockefeller (their son Nelson was a member of the Dartmouth class of 1930), Orozco was brought to Dartmouth in the spring of 1932 to exercise his skill as a painter and, through his painting, to teach. To the credit of Packard and Lathrop, and that of the college librarian, Nathaniel L. Goodrich, Orozco was encouraged to paint where he wished: not in Carpenter, but on the great expanse of plaster wall in the reserve reading room of Baker Library, directly adjacent to Carpenter. Orozco was given a faculty appointment by the trustees, and for almost two years students were privileged to witness a great artist at work.

FIGURE 9 Hopkins Center, 1962, Wallace K. Harrison, architect.

Completed in February of 1934, *The Epic of American Civilization* (number 134) is one of the most important works by the artist and is arguably the finest mural in this country.

In 1935 Abby Aldrich Rockefeller, an indefatigable patron of contemporary artists and a founder of the Museum of Modern Art, New York, gave to the college over one hundred paintings, drawings, prints, and sculptures. The Rockefeller gift constituted Dartmouth's first important collection of modern art. In addition to numerous twentieth-century works, the Rockefeller gift also included examples of nineteenth-century painting and sculpture and of folk art (see numbers 110 and 104).

This proved to be the beginning of a series of major gifts of works of art to the college, a phenomenon that was chiefly due to the efforts of Churchill P. Lathrop. Appropriately, the gallery devoted to modern art in the new museum has been named in his honor. Without Churchill Lathrop, many of the important works that ultimately led to the construction of the Hood Museum of Art would never have come to Dartmouth.

Also in 1935, Ray Nash set up his influential graphic arts print shop in the basement of Baker Library. Associated with both the English and the art departments, Nash educated almost two

generations of Dartmouth students in the history and art of graphic design and printing. It is to his influence, as well as to the energetic collecting activities of Churchill Lathrop, that Dartmouth owes its extensive print holdings.

Within three decades after the opening of Carpenter Hall, its art galleries and related art storage areas could no longer accommodate the college's expanding collection. At the same time, a need had arisen for a performing arts facility. The result was Hopkins Center, where President John Sloan Dickey envisioned all the creative arts brought together under one roof for the purpose of mutual enrichment.

When Hopkins Center (fig. 9) opened in the fall of 1962, it contained new facilities not only for theater and music, but for the visual arts as well. Designed by Wallace K. Harrison, the center contained studio space for what had become a curricular studio art program, as well as additional gallery, storage, and preparation areas for an increasingly active program of special exhibitions. This time the galleries were purposely placed in the mainstream of student life: students had to pass them to get to their mailboxes and to the center's snack bar. The visual arts had attained visibility at last.

1962–1985
TOWARD A UNIFIED MUSEUM

The improved visibility of art in the Hopkins Center galleries had dramatic consequences for the growth of the art collection and for the visual arts at Dartmouth in general; however, the migration of the gallery operation had other effects as well. While the administration of the galleries was incorporated into the activities of a lively performing arts center, the art history faculty and the art library remained across campus in Carpenter Hall. Inevitably, this administrative change resulted in a shift of emphasis away from the curricular concerns of scholars in the humanities and social sciences. Moreover, although Hopkins Center provided new storage space for the college's growing art collection, the galleries in Hopkins were used primarily for special exhibitions, while exhibition space for the permanent collection remained in Carpenter Hall. The result was a virtually untenable situation in which fragile works of art had to be transported back and forth across campus and subjected to wear and weather.

The creation of the Hopkins Center Art Galleries also had unforeseen consequences for the rest of Dartmouth's museum collections. Works of ethnographic interest, which during an earlier era would have been given to the anthropology collection of the College Museum in Wilson Hall, now tended to be given as art objects to the Hopkins Center Art Galleries. At the same time, curricular interest in the natural history collection of the College Museum had virtually disappeared.

When an economic recession threatened college resources during the early 1970s, the college administration initiated an evaluation of the museum and gallery operations at Dartmouth. In late 1974 it was decided that the college should divest itself of its natural history collection. Early the following year, an agreement was reached with Dr. Robert Chaffee, director of the College Museum, allowing him to use the college's natural history collection to found a regional museum in the Hanover area: the now-thriving Montshire Museum of Science. Even so, the remaining operations of the Dartmouth College Museum and Galleries remained widely scattered. Five exhibition and three storage areas were in three separate buildings, and the museum offices and work space were divided between Wilson Hall and Hopkins Center. The need for a new facility had become obvious.

In 1976 the college initiated a major fund-raising campaign for the arts at Dartmouth as part of an overall capital campaign. At that time Peter Smith, then the director of Hopkins Center, effectively stated the challenge that faced the college.

Dartmouth lacks the one thing that would give to the study and display of the fine arts what the Hopkins Center has so conspicuously given to the performing arts and the Visual Studies program—space commensurate with achievement and need, and a focus for increased attention. Until a new center is built devoted to the exhibition and contemplation of works of art, Dartmouth will not be able adequately to teach its students the kind of connoisseurship and visual discrimination which can make the crucial difference for artist and art historian alike, as well as for the future patron, collector, critic, trustee or curator. Students in major metropolitan areas have many museums to choose from for the prolonged and intensive study of works of art; almost all other institutions of Dartmouth's caliber outside of large cities have their own facilities sufficiently large, adaptable and well-protected to exhibit many of their treasures as well as major special shows. In addition to the effect on visual education at Dartmouth, a new museum would immediately become, as the Hopkins Center has, a great regional resource, affecting the much broader community beyond the College. And such museums consistently attract generous new gifts of art.

It is because so much has already been accomplished, because so much more is possible, that there is such unanimity among all who engage in any way in the study of the fine arts at Dartmouth in concentrating on the acquisition of a worthy new museum and study center. Nothing less will meet the need.[32]

The funding to meet this goal was assured in 1978, when the college received a bequest for a "major educational facility" from Harvey P. Hood. A member of the Dartmouth class of 1918, Harvey Hood had served the college as a trustee from 1941 to 1967. He had been an advisor to two Dartmouth presidents: Ernest Martin Hopkins, for whom Hopkins Center is named, and his successor, John Sloan Dickey, who was largely responsible for the concept of Hopkins Center as a meeting place for all the arts. This major bequest was augmented by additional gifts from members of the Hood family and from other generous supporters of the arts at Dartmouth.

As of September 28, 1985, the new Hood Museum of Art at Dartmouth College is open to the public. While it is a long-awaited moment, this history should make it clear that there is no intention of a dramatic break with the past. As anyone who knows Dartmouth knows well, tradition plays an essential role in the daily life of the college. Parts of the handsome and venerable "philosophical apparatus" that formed the core of the original eighteenth-century museum collection are displayed in Fairchild Science Center. There, much as in Dartmouth Hall almost two centuries ago, they are lovingly installed alongside works of art. The installation is a visible reminder of Dartmouth's sustained commitment to the totality of human knowledge—the belief that, given a broad enough perspective, the seemingly opposite horizons of science and art can be seen as continuous.

Likewise, many of the best college portraits are still on view in the Dartmouth College Library, alongside the books that have been their companions throughout their history.

The galleries in Carpenter Hall have been transformed into classrooms for the departments of art history and anthropology. There is a decorous symmetry in the fact that the anthropologists have joined the art historians there, just as the former anthropology collection has joined the art collection in the new museum. Wilson Hall, whose cornerstone-laying ceremony a century ago provoked a prediction that "before long, some one will affix his name to an Art Gallery totally distinct," is now one of the loveliest parts of the arts complex. It houses offices and classrooms

for the drama and film studies program, as well as administrative offices for Hopkins Center and the Hood Museum.

The museum itself is now an independent entity, free to develop the resources necessary to serve its diverse audience of students, scholars, and the general public. Yet the Hood Museum also retains important physical links to Hopkins Center, where its former exhibition galleries acquire new uses in the service of students and faculty in Dartmouth's Visual Studies Department.

Clearly, much has been accomplished during the five-year period that has seen the advent of a new president of the college, David T. McLaughlin, and a new provost, Agnar Pytte. The appointment of Charles W. Moore as architect of the new museum has proved to be a particularly happy decision for the college. Moore's academic career has been as distinguished as his career as a practicing architect. The holder of a Bachelor of Architecture degree from the University of Michigan and a Ph.D. from Princeton University, Moore has served as professor and chairman in the departments of architecture both at the University of California and at Yale. Since 1976 he has been professor and program head of architecture at the School of Architecture and Urban Planning of the University of California at Los Angeles. Recently he accepted an endowed chair in architecture at the University of Texas, Austin. Moore is the founder of several architectural firms, and he has published five books and dozens of articles on architectural theory and practice.

Charles Moore's familiarity with the academic environment, combined with his responsiveness to traditional forms, made him the perfect choice for Dartmouth's new museum. In the essay that follows, he recalls the active involvement of the college community in the building's planning, and he recounts the crucial decisions behind its design. Above all, the Hood Museum of Art was intended from the beginning to serve as a "good neighbor" within Dartmouth's distinguished architectural setting. This is especially fitting for the home of a collection whose history has been so richly and continuously interwoven with that of the college itself.

NOTES

1. The records of the meetings of the Dartmouth College trustees (Dartmouth College Archives), August 26, 1772: "Desired that his Excellency the Governor [Royal Governor Wentworth was a trustee of the college] return the Thanks of this Board to the Honorable John Phillips Esq. of Exeter for his generous donation of one hundred and seventy five Pounds lawful money recd. this day to assist in procuring a Philosophical Apparatus for this College."

2. McClure Collection, Dartmouth College Library. This letter is reproduced as a frontispiece in W. Wedgwood Bowen, *A Pioneer Museum in the Wilderness* (Hanover, Dartmouth College Museum, 1958). Bowen's extensive research notes for his booklet were a valuable resource in the writing of the present history. I would also like to acknowledge Gregory Schwarz's additions to Bowen's findings and especially Churchill P. Lathrop's article "To Promote Interest and Education in Art," *Dartmouth Alumni Magazine*, January 1951, pp. 12–18, 82–84.

3. Bowen, p. 35.

4. For examples of other early college art collections, see Jean C. Harris, *Collegiate Collections 1776–1876* (South Hadley, Mass., Mount Holyoke College, 1976).

5. *Diary of David McClure 1748–1820*, with notes by Franklin B. Dexter (New York, Knickerbocker Press, 1899), pp. 103, 150–51.

6. *Diary of David McClure*, p. 97.

7. David McClure and Elijah Parish, *Memoirs of the Rev. Eleazar Wheelock* (Newburyport, Mass., Edward Little and Co., 1811), p. 97.

8. Trustees' Records, May 26, 1773.

9. Trustees' Records, August 27, 1779.

10. Trustees' Records, September 20, 1782.

11. Baxter Perry Smith, *The History of Dartmouth College* (Boston, Houghton, Osgood and Co., 1878), pp. 78–79.

12. Frederick Chase, *A History of Dartmouth College and the Town of Hanover*, ed. John K. Lord (Cambridge, Mass., John Wilson and Son, 1891), pp. 573–74.

13. Trustees' Records, April 20, 1784: "The President laid before the board a letter from Governor Wentworth to him . . . on the subject of the donation of the Honorable John Phillips LLD for the procuring of a mathematical and philosophical apparatus, . . . the President having informed this board that William Rose of Cheswick LLD; and Paul Wentworth of Hammersmith, . . . from motives of generosity and benevolence, have undertaken by their own liberality and that of their friends to provide and transmit to America the next summer an apparatus for said College. And Doctor Phillips the donor of the sum deposited in Governor Wentworth's hands as before mentioned for procuring an apparatus having been consulted on the subject of an appropriation of his said donation under present prospects in respect to an apparatus by the hands of Dr. Rose and Mr. Paul Wentworth, and having expressed his willingness that it be applied to the procuring of books for the Library."

14. Chase, p. 222.

15. Trustees' Records, August 27, 1790: "Voted . . . that the middle apartment on the second storey in the front of the new building be accomodated for reception of the College library, . . . that the middle apartment in the third storey in the front of the new building be accomodated for the reception of the College apparatus to be removed there so soon as accomodations for it there can be made: and that the executive authority form suitable & proper regulations respecting it as they may from time to time find expedient."

16. John King Lord, *A History of Dartmouth College 1815–1909* (Concord, N.H., The Rumford Press, 1913), p. 607.

17. Dartmouth College Archives 795475.3.

18. *Diary of David McClure*, p. 48.

19. Leon Burr Richardson, *History of Dartmouth College*, 2 vols. (Hanover, Dartmouth College Publications, 1932), pp. 251–52.

20. Lord, p. 601; see also Gregory Schwarz, "Save the Zebra! Save the Zebra!" in the *Dartmouth Alumni Magazine*, February 1978, pp. 23–25.

21. The "Inspector of the College building [Dartmouth Hall]" was at the same meeting instructed to "proceed to finish and fit the room No. 4 on the lower storey for the reception of the Portraitures and the Apparatus"; however, later accounts seem to indicate that this transfer was never completely effected.

22. Lord, pp. 607–8.

23. *Echoes from Dartmouth*, ed. H. G. Hapgood ('96) and Craven Laycock ('96) (Hanover, 1895), p. 14.

24. James Bartlett Papers, Dartmouth College Library, 811652. I would like to acknowledge the diligence of Gregory Schwarz, whose research uncovered this letter.

25. Jim Halbe, "In This Corner," ed. H. T. Enns, Jr., *Fort Pierce* [Fla.] *News-Tribune*, April 27, 1950.

26. Lord, p. 608.

27. The Trustees' Records of July 26, 1836, mention a "Gallery of Paintings of this Institution."

28. John B. Stearns, *Reliefs from the Palace of Ashurnasirpal II* (Graz, Ernst F. Weidner, 1961), p. 8.

29. Stearns, p. 12. I would like to thank Judith Lerner, whose research on Dartmouth's Assyrian reliefs is being published separately.

30. This and the preceding quotation are taken from Lathrop, pp. 16–17.

31. From the copy of the Last Will and Testament of Ralph Butterfield, M.D., in the Dartmouth College Archives.

32. From *A Program of Support for the Arts at Dartmouth*, May 1976.

PLANNING THE HOOD MUSEUM OF ART

BY CHARLES W. MOORE

THE crucial issues involved in the planning of the Hood Museum of Art surfaced before we became its architects. Even in early 1981, when several firms were being considered for the commission, there was great uncertainty about the site of the building. The Hood was meant to be next to the Hopkins Center, working in close connection with it, but no site seemed ideal. In fact, I had been introduced to the problem of siting the Hood a year before. James Stirling, the eminent British architect who was teaching at Yale, had assigned the problem of the Hood to his students. I sat on the jury. It struck me that although many sites were available, there seemed to be no correlation between the site chosen and the excellence of the buildings produced in the student problem. Buildings that were placed on what seemed eminently logical and correct sites often lacked qualities manifest in buildings on less obvious sites.

When Dartmouth selected our firm to design the Hood Museum, my experience as a juror had already persuaded me that there was some virtue in not making a highly organized decision about which site to select. It seemed best to hold a kind of architectural beauty contest, in which we took advantage of our capacity to produce schemes quickly. We decided to design a building for each of the available sites and then discover which found the most favor. The task of selection was vested in a committee of about thirty people, representing many of the groups who were interested in the building. It was guided (with amazing skill and subtlety, I thought) by Leonard Rieser, who was then provost, and Peter Smith, director of Hopkins Center at that time. We set up shop in a room adjacent to the snack bar in the Hopkins Center, at the heart of comings and goings on campus. Our goal was to be, as much as we could, the opposite of mysterious: we wanted to be continuously available. We did this for weeks at a time, working on alternative schemes and welcoming the visits and intervention of anyone who was interested. We established ourselves as willing to talk. This receptivity is at the heart of our beliefs as architects, and it is one of our strengths. We are interested in listening, and in responding to people's images and ideas about the buildings they are to occupy. By now we have become fairly adept at picking up and making use of the things people tell us.

Our procedure began with devising schemes for six sites, which were then considered by the committee of thirty. (They came to be known as "The Gang of Thirty.") We were asked to forget a couple of the sites and to make an alternative to another of them, leaving us with five sites for the next round. We projected buildings for each of these, describing them with plans and models. People from our office were turning out models at high speed. These were all looked at, reconsidered, and rejected or accepted, until finally we were down to three schemes on three different sites.

The proceedings then began to resemble what I imagine a Republican convention might have been like in the 1880s. The museum's face onto the Green had always been an issue of great importance in discussions of the site. We had one site to the right of the theater entrance of Hopkins Center, as you look at it from the Green, and one to the left, between Hopkins and Wilson Hall. The committee had also retained a third possible site, a dark horse indeed, which was down the walk toward the courtyard between Hopkins Center and Brewster Hall, a dormitory to the south. At the time, it seemed most likely that the party favoring the building to the right of the Hop (thereafter known as "Tweedle Dum") would find common cause with the party favoring the building to the left (thereafter known as "Tweedle Dee"). Thus a compromise between the best of each might have

Charles W. Moore (seated, center) and Centerbrook architects Chad Floyd (left), Glen Arbonies (right), and Jim Childres (standing) with a model of the Hood Museum of Art, 1981.

occurred. No such luck. Again, it was like a political convention: the people in favor of one site could not see any virtue in the other, and vice versa. When the smoke cleared, the site tucked back in the center of the block had surfaced as the only one that made sense. The building was brought up to the Green by a connecting link between Wilson and the Hop, with an entrance and a sign, and was nestled among all the pieces of a very complicated block. I find it a fascinating choice, and I am delighted with it. Everyone on the committee seemed to be delighted when we arrived at it. Yet it is a choice that I am sure no one would have thought to leap straight to at the beginning of the design process.

Then we came to the issues of image and style. Now that we had a site, what might this building look like? At Dartmouth, of course, there are a number of historically important styles of building. Perhaps the one that is most powerful in people's minds is the big white "clapboard" Colonial, with gable roof, small windows, and green shutters. Several important Dartmouth buildings are in this style. Then there are the buildings of the later nineteenth century—the chapel, for example. At Dartmouth these tend to be quirky and very special—not pretentious and not staid, but wonderful, almost goofy little buildings that I am particularly fond of. Wilson Hall, which was built in 1885 as the library and president's office, is a particularly delightful example. Dartmouth also has a number of neo-Georgian buildings from the early twentieth century. These are at once traditional and calm, and in some cases (like Baker Library) extremely handsome, grand, and at times even bombastic in their quiet New England reticence. Twenty years ago, the Hopkins Center appeared in this setting. This important American building, one of the two or three masterworks of the architect Wallace K. Harrison, may have been the model for Harrison's Metropolitan Opera House in New York's Lincoln Center.

The Hood Museum, then, was to go between Hopkins Center and Wilson Hall. Now, the Hop is of an age that makes it extremely difficult for the architect. The building is full of heartfelt principles of planning, design, and style of exactly one generation before. It

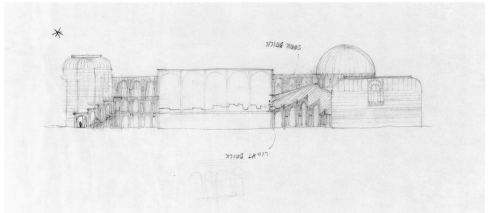

Early sketches by Charles Moore for the Hood Museum.

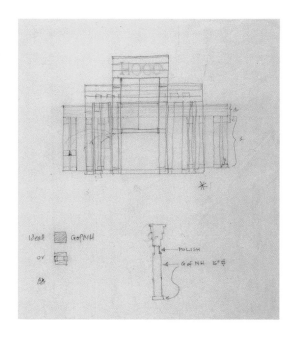

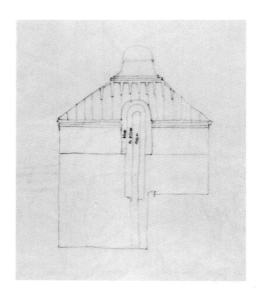

Early sketches by Charles Moore for the Hood Museum.

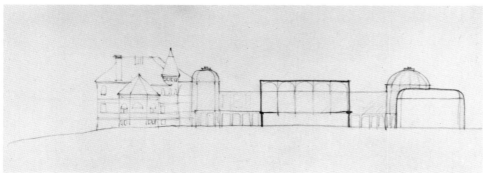

Wilson Hall and Hopkins Center, with the Hood Museum under construction between them, November 1984.

is easy for me to love Wilson. It is just far enough in the past to have romance and wonder, and I find it a charming building. But the Hop has a kind of assertiveness about it, an insistence—with its barrel vaults and modern shapes—that we are now in the midst of reacting against. Even so, it is a building of great conviction and power. To be churlish about its stylistic concerns would certainly be unbecoming. Here is a building not to copy, any more than we would want to copy Wilson, but to try to be a good neighbor to. Indeed, one of the tasks of the Hood is to be a good neighbor—to Hopkins Center, to Wilson, to the other buildings around, to the Green, and to the entire campus. Our task was to mediate between these very different architectural persuasions.

The best solution in this effort of mediating, it seemed to us, was a building that did not have one big overpowering image, but rather a number of images (perhaps smaller in scale, but not necessarily) that one would come upon in the course of wandering towards and through it. The first of these is the gate facing the Green. Next, we were interested in having a big room, something that you could remember when you went back to New York and thought about your visit to the Hood. In that room, we felt there should be some natural light from the top (not falling directly on the paintings, of course), and there should be a way to reach and adjust the lights up high, to make it easy to work with the place. We decided on a skylight with a catwalk running beneath. We also had occasion for flights of stairs to become important things to look at and to remember. In the choice of the site, we acquired a connection with the Hopkins Center snack bar in an area that we were able to enlarge and reshape, making it one of the festive gateways to the Hood.

Within the museum, we were excited by the prospect of organizing some of the small rooms into an equivalent of the long gallery in a stately British home of the sixteenth or seventeenth century. This series of smaller rooms—for works from the permanent collection or for temporary shows—provided a vista down the length of the gallery. Thus the

GROUND FLOOR

A The Arthur M. Loew Auditorium
B The Sanders Seminar Room
C The Barrows Print Room

FIRST FLOOR

D Lobby
E The Ivan Albright Gallery
F The Gene Y. Kim, Class of 1985, Gallery
G The Alvin P. Gutman Gallery
H The Israel Sack Gallery
I Conservation area
J Offices

SECOND FLOOR

K The Harrington Gallery
L The Churchill P. Lathrop Gallery
M The William B. Jaffe and Evelyn A. Jaffe Hall Galleries
N Friends Gallery
O The Owen Robertson Cheatham Gallery

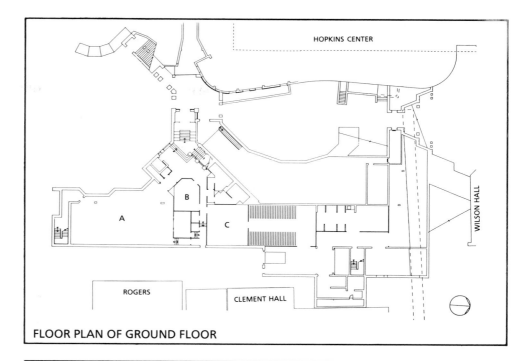

FLOOR PLAN OF GROUND FLOOR

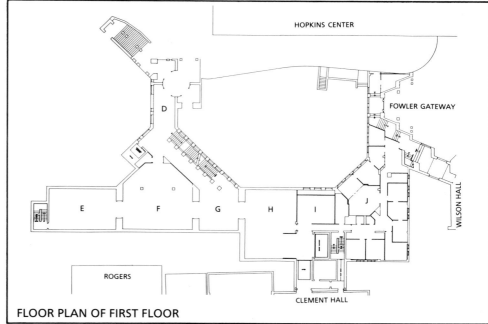

FLOOR PLAN OF FIRST FLOOR

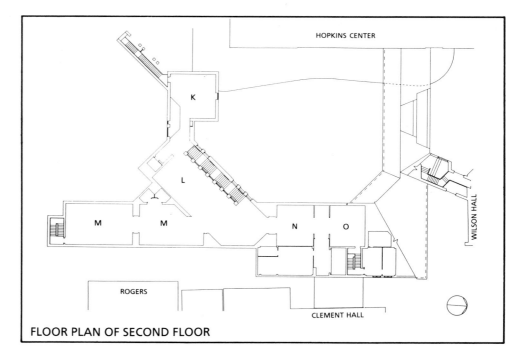

FLOOR PLAN OF SECOND FLOOR

Several views of the Hood Museum under construction, May 1985, including details of the cupola and cornice.

whole would be considerably more than the sum of its parts, but the parts would also be special. Among my favorite museums are the little ones with lots of special places—like the Phillips in Washington. I wanted this museum to be a series of rooms of very different proportions, grandeurs, and characters, where the art would not just appear in some anonymous matrix but would have the opportunity to enjoy its own environment.

As for the fabric of the building itself, we were extremely anxious to make it solid, and we chose brick. We would have loved it if some of the building could have been granite, expressive of our location in New Hampshire, but that was unaffordable this late in the twentieth century. We settled for bush-hammered concrete—not quite as everlasting but very close.

For the main section of the building, we liked the idea of a big vertical piece, like a New Hampshire industrial building, given a certain layer of civilization by the copper roof. We were also concerned to introduce some distinguishing feature that would not break up the solidity of that vertical mass surrounded by the less vertical masses. We settled on a cornice band—in gray brick, as it turned out, with a green-painted wooden cornice above. It looks so simple and inevitable, but of all the details

on the building, it was the one that received the most attention and even, at times, the most worry. We needed a material that would be distinctive without being showy. It also had to have permanence, unlike the glazed brick we once thought of using, which in some terrible cases was spalling and destroying itself in climates like that of Hanover. But the expressive possibilities of ornamental brick intrigued us. It is obviously not what you find on every post office building, nor, for that matter, on every academic building. We welcomed the chance to vary its dimensions, to make suggestions about what lies within—suggestions that were not meant to be too specific or to occasion too much wondering. Another fascinating task, also extremely difficult, was coordinating the green of the wooden cornice with the color of the copper roof as it now is and as it will become in time.

The style of the Hood Museum was not intended to be an assertion of a new idiom, as complete and on its own as the Hopkins Center had been in its day, and I would have been very upset if it had tried to be. I would have been equally upset if the new building had tried to ape any of the other persuasions that surround it. By the device of making a few things particularly ours—the cornice and the cupola, for instance—and by the interesting shapes and spaces that are, I hope, attractive to move into and through, we allowed the

building to develop its own special character. We were seeking something that supports and mediates between the fascinating buildings that lie around it. With any luck, the Hood will enhance all those other buildings and will make them even more fascinating.

I have some friends in New York who have a name for this kind of style—or non-style. They call it "free style," which is an interesting way of considering it. But it also misses, because it suggests that you can just do anything that comes into your head. We like to think that making something that enhances everything around it is not that easy. Maybe it has to do with animating the familiar, with bringing to life a set of things that strike chords of familiarity in us. This may call for shapes that are not exactly like what we are used to, but are close enough to it that we, the inhabitants, can feel as though the building is ours.

Centerbrook
Essex, Connecticut

An earlier discussion of the Dartmouth project appears in Helen Searing, *New American Art Museums* (New York and Berkeley: Whitney Museum of American Art and University of California Press, 1982), pp. 123–26.

**TREASURES OF
THE HOOD MUSEUM OF ART**
DARTMOUTH COLLEGE

ANCIENT ART

THE centerpiece of the art collection at Dartmouth is the set of Assyrian reliefs from the palace of Ashurnasirpal II, dating from the ninth century B.C. In quality, the Dartmouth reliefs are second only to those at the British Museum, and no other college or university collection has as many panels. Negotiations for acquisition of the reliefs began in 1853, but since they had to be sliced from the foot-thick wall in six-inch-thick slabs, cut into sections, and carried across the desert by camel to a Lebanese port, the reliefs did not arrive in Hanover until December 11, 1856. The acquisition can be credited to the joint efforts of three men: Dartmouth professor Oliver Hubbard, who initiated the transaction, the Reverend Austin H. Wright, and the Reverend Henry Lobdell (see also pages 14–15). Sir Henry Creswicke Rawlinson, the British archaeologist who secured the reliefs for Wright, was given an honorary degree by the college in 1857.

The first mention of ancient "curiosities" at Dartmouth occurs in an 1810 inventory of early college acquisitions. The list includes a marble segment from a temple of Serapis and two fragments of Pompey's Pillar from a Mr. Dinsmore. The collection of Frederick Hall, which came in 1838, also included Egyptian and Roman material. The Hall artifacts, numbering about ten, are of slight scholarly interest today, but they are good examples of the curios collected in the early nineteenth century.

The first major collection of antiquities came to the college in 1912 from Mrs. Hiram Hitchcock. The Hitchcock Bequest included 456 Cypriote objects and 95 artifacts collected in Egypt. Shortly after 1858 Hiram Hitchcock, a resident of Hanover and New York City, had met and become close friends with Luigi Palma di Cesnola, a collector of antiquities and later director of the Metropolitan Museum of Art in New York. Cesnola, a brigadier general in the Civil War, had become the United States consul to Cyprus in 1865, a time when antiquities there were receiving great attention. After eleven years on the island, he had amassed the largest collection of Cypriote antiquities in the world. Hitchcock acquired a number of items from Cesnola, including the *Head of a Bearded Votary* (number 3), as well as a fine collection of glass and pottery from Cyprus. This group of objects, though uneven in quality, joined the

Assyrian reliefs to form the core of the collection of ancient art at Dartmouth.

The museum also has its requisite Egyptian mummy, brought from Egypt by William Ephraim Morris of Hartford, Vermont, and presented to Dr. William T. Smith, dean of the Medical School. The Dartmouth mummy is that of an adolescent boy and dates from about 700 B.C. The invoice for the mummy, dated 1894, indicates that it was excavated fifty yards from the pyramid of Hawara-el-Maktaa.

The first purchase in the area of ancient art was made in 1923, when two sets of Babylonian tablets, which had been on loan to the collection for eight years, were acquired permanently. In 1930 Mrs. Maribel Pratt, wife of Elon Graham Pratt, class of 1906, presented Dartmouth with a collection of Egyptian amulets. These fifty-five objects are representative of the types, subjects, and materials common among Egyptian amulets from the early dynasties to Roman days.

Ray Winfield Smith, of the class of 1918, donated three of Dartmouth's most important ancient objects: the Egyptian lion head (number 2), the Panathenaic amphora (number 5), and a kylix dated to the sixth century B.C. and attributed to the Epidromos Painter. Although Smith was distinguished primarily as a scholar and collector of ancient glass, his collection had a wide range. His gifts enriched the museum in other areas as well and include a predella panel attributed to the Master of the Bambino Vispo (number 53).

Another significant gift of ancient art—four Early Christian mosaics from Homs in Syria (number 6)—came into the Dartmouth collection through the generosity of D. Herbert Beskind, who also played a key role in building the holdings of Asian art (see numbers 7, 8, 10, and 11).

A recent acquisition is the third-century Roman sarcophagus pictured in this section (number 4). Thanks to purchases and donations such as this, the collection has gained a depth for study and a range for display that touch on much of the ancient world.   H.B.

a

b

1
Assyrian, reign of Ashurnasirpal II, 883–859 B.C.

Reliefs from the Northwest Palace of Ashurnasirpal II at Nimrud

a. *Attendant to the King*, 93 × 42 in. (236.2 × 106.7 cm)

b. *The King and Genie*, 93 × 85 in. (236.2 × 215.9 cm)

c. *Genie with Pail and Date-Palm Spathe*, 91½ × 51 in. (232.4 × 129.6 cm)

d. *Wingless Genie with Pail*, 90 × 39 in. (228.6 × 99.1 cm)

e. *Winged Genie with Pail*, 90½ × 58 in. (229.8 × 147.4 cm)

f. *Genie Annointing a Sacred Tree*, 92 × 85½ in. (233.7 × 217.2 cm)

Gypsum

Gift of Sir Henry Rawlinson through Austin H. Wright, Class
of 1830

S.856.3.1–6

1 In 1856 Dartmouth College acquired six bas-relief panels that once decorated the palace of Ashurnasirpal II in the ancient city of Calah in Assyria. Austen Henry Layard discovered the site at Calah, the modern city of Nimrud, Iraq, and began excavations there in 1845. Between 1850 and 1860 approximately fifty-five panels were exported to the United States for study, the majority going to colleges. At Dartmouth, Professor Oliver P.

Hubbard asked the Reverend Austin H. Wright, a member of the class of 1830 and a missionary in the area, to negotiate on behalf of the college. Wright was able to secure for Dartmouth a fine set of panels through Sir Henry Rawlinson, a British archaeologist working at the site (see also pages 14–15).

The Dartmouth panels depict a beardless attendant to the king, with quiver, bow, sheathed sword, and a scepter decorated with a rosette; King Ashurnasirpal II with

bow and arrows, followed by a winged, human-headed genie who serves as his cupbearer and who anoints the king with a date-palm spathe; a genie with a pail holding a date-palm spathe; a wingless genie; a winged genie; and a winged genie pollinating a date tree. This sacred Tree of Life is the central symbol of the spiritual odyssey depicted in the palace. The theme of these

b

reliefs, the symbolic fertilization of the date palm, is shown not only because the tree provided the Assyrians with food, drink, and shelter, but also because the date palm was for them a direct manifestation of the magic of nature. Through the decoration of the palace with these motifs, the power of the symbols was associated with the ruler. These two themes, the glory of the king and the wonder of the Tree of Life, are central to the iconographic program of the palace.   H.B.

2
Egyptian, New Kingdom, c. 1559–1085 B.C.
Lion Head (Sekhmet)
Stone, h. 13 in. (33.0 cm),
diam. 13¾ in. (35.0 cm)
Gift of Mr. and Mrs. Ray Winfield Smith,
Class of 1918
S.975.6

2 This lion head, of gray-black schist, is probably a fragment of a Middle Kingdom representation of Sekhmet. A goddess capable of causing or curing illness, Sekhmet was represented as a composite figure, half woman and half lioness, usually seated. She was popular in the Memphis region of ancient Egypt and was invoked in times of plague. The rough texture of the headdress is an indication that a Middle Kingdom inscription or design may have been removed to be replaced by another during the New Kingdom.   H.B.

3
Cypriote
Head of a Bearded Votary, c. 480 B.C.
Limestone, h. 15½ in. (39.4 cm),
diam. 9⅝ in. (24.5 cm)
Bequest of Mrs. Hiram Hitchcock,
from the Luigi Palma di Cesnola Collection
12-1-324

4
Roman, Early Antonine
Sarcophagus Fragment with Eros, Nereids, Tritons, and a Sea Horse, c. 140–160
Marble, 18½ × 47¼ × 4 in. (47.0 × 120.0 × 10.2 cm)
Inscribed lower center: *NHRE[I]DES*
Acquisitions from Gifts Reserve Fund
S.977.21

3 This wreathed Cypriote head, characteristic of the early Severe Style of Greek sculpture and reminiscent of the Zeus of Artemisium in the National Museum in Athens, shows Assyrian influence in the stylized cap of hair and beard, the slight archaic smile, and the high cheekbones. The wreath represents laurel over ivy and berries. The nose has been restored and is broader than the original. Characteristic of early Greek sculpture, this head once was brightly painted: traces of buff-colored pigment appear in the eyes, and blue paint survives in the drill borings of the beard.   H.B.

4 This sarcophagus fragment was acquired by Thomas Herbert, eighth earl of Pembroke (1654–1732), and was recorded in the seventeenth century as forming part of his collection at Wilton House. The Nereid (a water nymph) on the far right leads a sea horse who struggles to be released; her arm is held by a Triton (a merman) who is supporting the central Nereid; Eros, holding a wreath, follows behind. The Nereid (or Venus?) on the far left holds a hoofed Triton in an unusual, abandoned embrace. This pose has been noted for showing a blend of Italian and Eastern influences. The word

"Nereids," a later addition, is inscribed in post-fifteenth-century Greek on the lower edge of the marble slab. As decoration for a sarcophagus, the watery theme may allude to the salvation and rebirth of a Christian soul from the waters of baptism, a translation of mythological imagery to Christian symbolism in the late Roman period.   H.B.

5
The Berlin Painter, Greek, sixth to fifth century B.C.
Panathenaic Amphora, c. 500–475 B.C.
Terra-cotta, h. 24½ in. (62.2 cm)
Inscribed vertically: *TONATHENETHTHENATHLON*
[Of the prizes at Athens]
Gift of Mr. and Mrs. Ray Winfield Smith,
Class of 1918
C.959.53

5 Amphorae often were given as prizes at the Panathenaic games held yearly in Athens on the birthday of the goddess Athena. This black-figure amphora, inscribed "Of the prizes at Athens," is thought to have contained sacred olive oil. Painted by the Berlin Painter—so named because a magnificent amphora by this master is in Berlin—the vessel is decorated on one side with the traditional figure of Athena Polias standing between two Doric columns surmounted by cocks. The reverse side, which has usually been described as a representation of wrestlers, may instead depict *pankratists*, contenders in a combined boxing and wrestling event.   H.B.

a. *Rampant Dog in a Flying Gallop*, 42½ × 70¾ in. (107.9 × 180.0 cm)

b. *Four-part Panel with Birds,
Façade, and Boat*,
54 × 54⅞ in. (137.1 × 139.4 cm)

c. *Fish, Peacock, and Lamb*,
64¼ × 36¼ in. (163.2 × 92.0 cm)

d. *Stag with Bird*,
40½ × 43⅝ in. (102.8 × 110.8 cm)
Mis.974.352–55

6
Early Christian, Syria
Mosaic Fragments, c. fifth to sixth century
Marble tesserae
Gift of Mr. and Mrs. D. Herbert Beskind,
Class of 1936

6 These four Early Christian mosaics from Homs, in Syria, are similar in style to those found at Antioch, a little more than a hundred miles away. The boldest of the panels, showing a rampant dog in a flying gallop, would have been part of a larger hunting scene. The early Christians associated the symbol of the hunt with the concept of duality—the triumph of good over evil. Originating from Near Eastern imperial hunt scenes and Roman pagan imagery, the theme of the hunt became popular in Early Christian art as its meaning was assimilated into Christian symbolism (see number 4).

The second panel is divided into four sections, the borders of which are executed in parallel rows of black and beige tesserae on a white background. The two upper sections have roundels enclosing images of birds. The bottom sections have images enclosed in triangles: on the left is a building façade of classical design; on the right is a boat, which appears to be a commercial vessel in full sail carrying cargo.

The third fragment shows a peacock, symbol of immortality, between two emblems of Christ: a fish at the top and a lamb at the bottom. The last shows a stag, typifying piety and religious aspiration, with a bird, symbol of the soul, resting on his back.   H.B.

ASIAN ART

THE gift of a large collection of Chinese paintings in 1942 encouraged Dartmouth to expand its holdings in Asian art. At that time the college received a share of the extensive Frederick Peterson Collection assembled over a period of many years by William Bingham II. The original collection consisted of 825 paintings and was stored at Princeton University. The cataloguing of these works was undertaken by Berthold Laufer in 1929, and they remained at Princeton until 1941, when Professors George Rowley and Frank Jewett Mather suggested that the collection be divided among five educational institutions. In addition to Dartmouth and Princeton, other recipients were Amherst, Bowdoin, and Williams colleges. Dartmouth's acquisitions from the Peterson Collection include a number of fine nineteenth-century albums containing ink-and-wash paintings on silk, various scroll paintings, and modern Chinese works.

Prior to 1942 the college museum held few examples of Far Eastern art, with the exception of a collection of objects from Southeast Asia, donated in 1939 by Mr. and Mrs. J. W. Barrett. This gift of artifacts from Siam (Thailand) consisted of silver pipes, knives, swords, ivory sculpture, brass, wood, and musical instruments. Although the subsequent growth of Dartmouth's collection has emphasized the decorative arts of China and Japan, the Barretts' Siamese material provided an impetus for expanding the holdings of the art of lesser-known cultures. In addition to the Southeast Asian pieces, the Hood collection now includes a limited number of Korean, Indian, and Tibetan objects.

The Hood Museum's Asian collection is strongest in the areas of ceramics and bronzes, attesting to the popularity of Far Eastern decorative arts among American collectors. This aspect of the collection owes much to the thoughtful gifts of Mr. and Mrs. D. Herbert Beskind, class of 1936, and Mr. and Mrs. William B. Jaffe, honorary members of the class of 1964. During the 1960s, Herbert Beskind served as chairman of the Art Advisory Committee at Dartmouth. Churchill P. Lathrop, then director of the galleries, informed him of the collection's needs in this area and how they might best be filled. As a result Beskind contributed significant Chinese bronzes, rounding out a collection that already included fine examples of vessels from the transitional period between the Shang and Chou dynasties. The Beskinds also donated a number of Indian sculptures, including a stele of Avalokiteśvara from the Pāla dynasty, as well as examples of Chinese painting.

Mr. and Mrs. William B. Jaffe, who have been instrumental in strengthening the modern and ethnographic areas of the collection, also expanded Dartmouth's resources in Chinese ceramics and Japanese prints. Many handsome pieces of Chinese porcelain came to the Hood Museum by way of the Jaffes, including such highlights as the celadon vase illustrated here (number 9), a tz'u-chou type sgraffito vase, a large blue-and-yellow glazed pilgrim bottle, and a famille rose enameled Imperial vase. Noting a significant lack of Japanese prints, paintings, and sculpture, the Jaffes responded by donating a series of woodcuts depicting courtesans by the Japanese printmaker Utagawa Toyokuni. In 1971 John C. Richardson augmented the holdings of Japanese prints with a gift in memory of his father, Edward C. Richardson, class of 1905: two complete sets of Hiroshige's Tokaido series, the Great Tokaido and the Reisho Tokaido (number 12).

Recent contributions to the Asian collection have continued to strengthen the museum's holdings. In 1980 Mr. and Mrs. James P. Todd gave the college a portion of their important family collection of ancient Chinese bronze mirrors (published by M. Rupert and O. J. Todd in Chinese Bronze Mirrors, 1935). Another recent addition came in 1981 in the form of a major gift of Chinese ceramics and pottery from Mrs. Patrick C. Hill. Among these objects are several pairs of molded T'ang dynasty tomb figurines and early tomb animals. In particular, a delicate female attendant glazed in white displays the simple beauty of Chinese sculpture.

The Hood Museum is also indebted to Dr. and Mrs. Lewis Balamuth for their contribution in 1968 of more than seventy jade carvings. Many pieces are deserving of mention, among them an oblong burial tablet carved in relief and a statuette of the Buddha of Good Fortune, Pū-tai.

As the development of the Hood Museum's collection continues, more attention is being given to the acquisition of Asian art. The most recent additions to the collection, two Ming fresco paintings and a Japanese Tosa screen, were presented in June 1984 by Jane and Richard Lombard, class of 1953.   L.P.Q.

7 Once used in ritual ceremonies for sacrificial offerings of meat or grain, this vessel dates from an early period of Chinese bronze production. A method of direct casting was used to produce this deep, circular container that rests on a foot ring and is characterized by zoomorphic handles. Below the rim is a frieze decorated with scrolls and two t'ao-t'ieh motifs (heads of apparently feline or bovine monsters). A six-character inscription that identifies for whom the vessel was made is cast inside on the bottom of the bowl. L.P.Q.

8 This hollow, kidney-shaped pillow is covered with a finely crackled cream glaze that has taken on a subtle light-brown tone, possibly due to water immersion. Records indicate that it may have been recovered at Chu lu-hsien, a market town in North China that was devastated by flood in 1108. The top surface is decorated with a large, skillfully written character symbolizing jen (tolerance) against a combed ground. The heavily incised lines in the cream-colored slip classify this piece as stoneware of the tz'u-chou type. L.P.Q.

7

Chinese, Western Chou Dynasty,
1027–771 B.C.
Meat or Grain Container (Kuei),
c. tenth century B.C.
Bronze, h. 5¼ in. (13.4 cm),
diam. 7⅝ in. (19.4 cm)
Inscription on interior of base
Gift of Mr. and Mrs. D. Herbert Beskind,
Class of 1936
M.961.269

8

Chinese, Sung Dynasty, 960–1279
Tz'u-chou Pillow, before 1108
Stoneware with sgraffito on cream slip,
5¼ × 12¾ × 9½ in.
(13.4 × 32.4 × 24.2 cm)
Gift of Mr. and Mrs. D. Herbert Beskind,
Class of 1936
C.957.155

9
Chinese, Northern Sung Dynasty,
960–1279
Vase
Porcelain with celadon glaze,
h. 32¼ in. (81.9 cm)
Gift of Evelyn A. and William B. Jaffe,
Class of 1964H
C.958.363

9 This unusually large beaker-form vase was formerly in the collection of Samuel Peters, a well-known collector of Chinese ceramics. Only two similar examples are known, both located in the Imperial Museum, Imperial Palace, Beijing. During the Sung dynasty, aesthetic preference in ceramic wares tended toward fine porcelain with monochrome glazes. The subtle blue-green glaze of celadon, a color produced only with great difficulty, was esteemed for its resemblance to jade. This piece is glazed overall with a pale blue-green celadon and is accented by thin black bands around the neck and body.   L.P.Q.

11
Chinese, T'ang Dynasty, 618–906
Groom Figurine
Earthenware with three-color glaze, h. 13¼ in. (33.7 cm)
Gift of Mr. and Mrs. D. Herbert Beskind, Class of 1936
S.957.144

10
Chinese, Ming Dynasty, 1368–1644
Dice Bowl, Hsüan-te period, 1426–35
Porcelain with underglaze blue, h. 4 in. (10.2 cm), diam. 11 in. (28.0 cm)
Inscribed on side with reign mark of Hsüan-te
Gift of Mr. and Mrs. D. Herbert Beskind, Class of 1936
C.958.369

10 The pure, simple form of this Ming dynasty bowl emphasizes the beauty of its cobalt-blue decoration against the white background. A delicate peony and leaf design is painted on the exterior with underglaze blue; the white interior is undecorated. The base of the bowl joins the foot rim amidst a circle of lotus panels, and the rim itself is embellished with a repeated flower design. Below the double line that borders the top edge, the six-character reign mark of Hsüan-te is written horizontally.　L.P.Q.

11 A fine example of a T'ang dynasty tomb figure, this foreign household servant (possibly an Armenian retainer) is rendered realistically with an unsophisticated charm. The inclusion of pottery figures in tombs was a practice common in China from the third century B.C. through the seventeenth century A.D. Most of these figures were produced in large quantities from molds and then decorated with three-color glazes. Our male servant is clad in a long, amber-brown coat with blue lapels. The mottled glaze on his boots probably was caused by fluid glazes that tended to run and mix during firing. L.P.Q.

12
Utagawa (Andō) Hiroshige, Japanese, 1797–1858
Hakone (number eleven from the Reisho Tokaido series), 1848–49
Color woodcut, impression 8½ × 13½ in. (21.6 × 34.3 cm)
Gift of John C. Richardson, Class of 1941, in memory of his father,
Edward C. Richardson, Class of 1905
Pr.972.64.11

12 Hiroshige is well known as the Japanese master of impressionistic, poetic views of nature. With the introduction of his numerous Tokaido Road series, he contributed a great deal to the development of Japanese landscape prints. This particular image is one of fifty-five prints from the series entitled Reisho Tokaido, so called because the title is written in *reisho*, or formal clerical script, on the red cartouche. Published by Marusei during the Prohibition period, the edition is extremely rare, as the woodblocks were destroyed after only a few impressions had been taken. This print, a scene of Hakone (one of the stations along the road between Edo and Kyoto), is number eleven in the series and depicts six men on foot, two of whom carry a seventh in a litter.　L.P.Q.

NATIVE AMERICAN ART

INDIAN art of the Americas claims proud, diverse, and ancient traditions that are integrally related to the long and complex history of the continents' first inhabitants. The pre-Columbian art traditions of Central and South America can be traced to the second millennium B.C., and they represent a continuum of changing forms and functions over 3,000 years. Originally big-game hunters, the Native American populations eventually adopted settled village life with the domestication of corn. In the continuity of this settled, agrarian existence the Indians of Central and South America began to elaborate their material culture and to enrich both life and death with articles of utility, adornment, and symbolic value. They communicated with their gods, and they built temples and pyramids in honor of the deities and those perceived as closest to them, the priest-kings. The grandeur of pre-Columbian America's monumental stone architecture has not been surpassed anywhere, while the smaller objects made of pottery, stone, gold, jade, and textile attest to a highly developed mastery of technique and an inventiveness of form and iconography. The momentum of these flourishing civilizations was arrested and, indeed, destroyed by conquest and colonial domination. Today it is the art—mostly retrieved by archaeology—that remains as a witness to the former splendor and coherence of a way of life that terminated soon after the advent of Europeans on the shores of the New World.

On the North American continent, the oldest Indian art traditions are those of the Southwest. Here corn-cultivating communities have maintained an unbroken tradition of pottery art from the late first millennium A.D. to the present. Evidence suggests that this development owed its stimulus to the ancient Mexican pottery traditions. The art of the later, Southeastern mound-building culture—which flourished between 1200 and 1500 as a major political, ceremonial, and trade center of native North America—also shows formal and iconographic similarities to Mesoamerican art.

The ranked societies of the Northwest developed an important tradition of wood carving in North America. Their art production is abundant with complex iconographic references to mythology and offers a dramatic visual manifestation of the Northwest Indians' conceptual relationship to the cosmos and the natural environment. The sheer richness of expression, its formal inventiveness, and its aesthetic coherence accord this work major status among world art traditions. First encountered by early explorers in the late eighteenth century, the antecedents of these traditions can now be dated to approximately 1000.

Everywhere, the specific historic circumstances of advancing European contact and domination caused change in Indian culture and art. In some areas, the Southwest for instance, such change worked slowly and was barely perceptible until the late nineteenth century; in other areas, notably the Northeast and the Plains, contact with Europeans provided the impetus for drastic shifts in the orientation of culture. The Plains Indian culture, for example, as it was encountered by the advancing white settlers from the East in the early nineteenth century, centered around the horse, a legacy of earlier Spanish exploration of the New World. In the Northeast the ready availability of European glass beads as articles of trade and the floral decorations on the clothing accessories used by the French Ursuline Sisters (a Catholic missionary order) provided the stimulus for a new aesthetic of beadwork. The new design was based on the indigenous curvilinear forms originally executed in porcupine quills, but in the medium of glass beads it soon evolved into larger and bolder naturalistic floral forms on fields of vividly contrasting colors. This artistic innovation rapidly diffused westward and eventually came to characterize and dominate the art of the Great Lakes region as well. By the turn of the twentieth century glass beads had largely replaced quills throughout the continent. Like artists anywhere, those of Native America accepted the challenge of new materials and experimented with new forms. Rarely, however, was their holistic aesthetic vision uncritically subjugated to a foreign aesthetic: forms and designs were adapted, but direct imitation was rare.

Native American art served the needs of its societies. It was as much an art of personal adornment, social prestige, individual valor, and domestic pursuit as it was a conduit to the supernatural, expressive of the Indians' spiritual affinity with the natural environment and forces of the universe. A profound respect for the condition of all phenomena, animate and inanimate, was pervasive in their concept of the world. They conceived of human beings as but one part of the interrelated energy of all things. It was therefore incumbent upon them to live as guests on the land, never abusing its nurturing qualities.

The harmonious integration of life and art in native North America fostered a condition in which anyone's potential to be an artist was acknowledged. While the production of articles of religious significance was reserved for religious specialists, the division of artisanship was generally drawn along gender lines. Women made pottery, basketry, textiles, and needlework, including that with quills and beads; men worked in wood, stone, bone, and metal. (An exception is the Southwest, where Pueblo men traditionally were the weavers.) Mastery of material and form—that unique achievement of aesthetic excellence—was praised and rewarded in native societies. Native American artists traditionally did not sign their works, but within their communities their names and reputations were well known and, though lost to us, would have equalled the recognition accorded the hand of a master anywhere.

The archaeological and ethnographic collections from Mesoamerica and North America at Dartmouth account for two-thirds (about 15,000 artifacts) of the total non-Western holdings. They include a high proportion of sculptural fragments, pottery shards, and undocumented lithic material. The first important donation of Native American material (purported to relate to Chief Joseph of the Nez Perce) was received from William Leeds in the 1880s. Other groups of objects were donated during the course of the present century, largely through the active network of well-traveled Dartmouth alumni. Their contributions were solicited or gratefully accepted by the Dartmouth College Museum, whose mission at the time was the encyclopedic documentation of world cultures.

With few exceptions, the artifacts collected by these individuals were neither assembled systematically nor obtained at the site of origin or use. Many of them were bought from traders as mementos of travelers' forays into "exotic" environments; consequently, documentation of their origins is gener-

ally lacking. Among the pre-Columbian materials from Central America at Dartmouth, the Victor M. Cutter Collection is an outstanding exception. Cutter, of the class of 1903, worked in Central America as a manager of the United Fruit Company from the time of his graduation until 1916. He was an avid collector and assembled a fine group of terra-cotta and stone objects from Guatemala, Honduras, Costa Rica, Panama, and Colombia. Most of these objects carry a designation of their place of origin.

For native North America the Frank C. and Clara G. Churchill Collection represents a comparable situation. Frank C. Churchill was a nineteenth-century local manufacturer and prominent civic leader who worked as Indian Inspector for the Department of the Interior from 1899 to 1909. Churchill traversed the continent in this capacity accompanied by his wife, Clara G. Churchill. Mrs. Churchill regularly collected artifacts from the more than one hundred Indian groups from the Southwest to Alaska that she and her husband visited. She also kept a diary in which she recorded—albeit inconsistently—collection locales, names of artists, owners of objects, purchase prices, and miscellaneous quaint stories. Mr. Churchill died in 1911. From 1921 through 1926 Mrs. Churchill was courted by the American Indian Heye Foundation for her collection. Dartmouth was a close rival, and by a stroke of fortune the entire collection came to the college in 1946 after Mrs. Churchill's death. The Churchill Collection is the backbone of Dartmouth's native North American ethnographic holdings, as it represents a majority of the native culture areas and is supported by a modicum of reliable documentation.

The character of the Churchill material resembles that of other smaller ethnographic collections at Dartmouth in that it is strong in the types of objects that

were readily accessible to the public. Pottery vessels, baskets, textiles, articles of clothing, and accessories abound. Around the turn of the century, when the Churchills collected, these articles were available for purchase, and many were made for sale and bought by Mrs. Churchill directly from the artisan (for example, number 22). Articles of ritual and religious significance, on the other hand, are almost totally absent from the Churchill Collection.

In terms of object types, baskets represent one of the strongest areas of the Dartmouth ethnographic holdings. In addition to those from the Churchill Collection, there is a comprehensive group of baskets from California, some of which were acquired at their site of origin in the late nineteenth century. The museum's Northwest Coast baskets include a Tlingit group from Axel Rasmussen, considered the last important collector of traditional artifacts of that area.

In general, the North American Indian collection at Dartmouth is distinguished by its representation of secular objects and characteristic examples of various culture areas, but it is rarely comprehensive for a given culture. The collection was assembled during the period when traditional native cultures were changing rapidly and was formed with the intent of documenting the remaining spectrum of material culture. Dartmouth's more recent focus on Native American art as a corollary to cultural documentation presents a new challenge to further build and extend our Native American collection.   T.N.

14
Mexico, Morelos, San Pablo(?),
Middle Preclassic, 1200–500 B.C.
Standing Female Figure
Terra-cotta with traces of white pigment, h. 11¼ in. (28.6 cm)
Gift of Evelyn A. and William B. Jaffe, Class of 1964H
S.965.56.4

13
Costa Rica, Guanacaste, Nicoya zone,
late Period VI, c. 1200–1400
Zoomorphic Effigy Vessel
Terra-cotta with pigment,
h. 8½ in. (21.6 cm)
Gift of Mrs. Victor M. Cutter
38.12.5442

13 Recent archaeological excavations have led to the ordering of pre-Columbian ceramics from Costa Rica into a new classification system. The vessel shown here, with its decoration of black and red on white pottery, is of the type formerly known as Nicoya Polychrome; today these vessels are called Pataky Polychrome. Their white surfaces are thought to indicate the influence of ceramic style from the north, the area of modern Nicaragua. The animal—whose head contains a clay bead that produces a rattling sound—probably represents a squirrel. The polychrome decoration includes a painted band around the vessel neck with stylized plumed-serpent motifs.   T.N.

14 Large, hollow ceramic figures of this type were among the mortuary offerings of the peoples living in the central highlands of Mexico during the early first millennium B.C. They varied in style from town to town. This figure, with its high, flat headdress, is similar to pieces found at the Morelos site called San Pablo, in what is believed to be a rare burial mound. The San Pablo pieces resemble figures that have been found in the Preclassic burial sites at Tlatilco in the Valley of Mexico. T.N.

17
Peru, Moche, Piura
Stirrup Spout Vessel, first to third century
Terra-cotta with traces of white pigment, h. 8 in. (20.3 cm)
Gift of Louise C. and Frank L. Harrington, Class of 1924
C.975.90

15 and 16
TOP LEFT AND LEFT
Guatemala, Maya, Quiriguá
Heads, 810
Sandstone; 15: h. 9½ in. (24.2 cm); 16: h. 11⅝ in. (29.5 cm)
Gift of Mrs. Victor M. Cutter
38.12.5537–8

15 and **16** These heads once decorated the middle doorway of the building now designated Structure 1B-1-1st, on the south side of the Temple Plaza at Quiriguá. The building is dated to 810 by a hieroglyphic inscription ("9.19.0.0.0."), which corresponds to the reign of the Quiriguá ruler Jade Sky. The heads were collected in 1911 during the Second Quiriguá Expedition of the School of American Archaeology.   T.N.

17 Effigy vessels of the early Moche style, such as this rather fierce monkey, have come in some quantity from burials in the northern Piura area of Peru. An important and artistically rich group of objects, their exact relationship to the early Moche art of the Pacific Coast, the home of the Moche people, is not clear at present.   T.N.

19
New Mexico, Zuni Pueblo
Ceremonial Vessel, nineteenth century
Terra-cotta with black and white pigment,
h. 4½ in. (11.5 cm), diam. 11⅝ in. (29.6 cm)
Gift of G. H. Browne
42.12.8110

18
New Mexico, Anasazi, Chaco—San Juan River area,
1000–1100
Pitcher
Terra-cotta with white and black pigment, h. 8 in. (20.3 cm)
Acquired by exchange with Mount Holyoke College Art Museum
55.37.13327

18 The ceramic art traditions of the South-western Pueblo farmers are rooted in the preceding Anasazi culture and can be traced to 100 B.C. The continuity of this ancient art—created by women—into the present attests to the vitality and cultural significance of these traditions. The prominent archetypal spiral motif on this vessel is found on many types of prehistoric pottery from the South-west.   T.N.

19 The sculptural quality of this bowl is created by the two pairs of stepped-cloud motifs defining its rim. The strict formal symmetry of the bowl's shape is further emphasized by the painted imagery of frogs and tadpoles in symmetric opposition. The symbols of stepped clouds, frogs, and tad-poles reflect the Pueblo farmers' deep con-cern with water, the essential and life-renewing element in their arid environment. Bowls of this type were used ceremonially to serve sacred corn meal.   T.N.

a

b

c

d

20
British Columbia, Haida(?)
Portrait Figures, nineteenth century
a. Wood, bone, black pigment,
h. 6⅞ in. (17.5 cm), 22.3.1880
b. Wood, bone, brown pigment,
h. 7½ in. (19.1 cm), 22.3.1941
c. Wood, bone, black pigment,
h. 5½ in. (14.0 cm), 22.3.1877
d. Wood, green and brown pigment,
h. 8½ in. (21.0 cm), 22.3.1883
Gift of Margaret Kimberly

20 Carved figures of various sizes—traditionally used by shamans or in ceremonial drama—were part of the standard repertoire of Northwest Coast art. Increased European and Euro-American contact eventually generated among the Haida and others another genre of statuary: small male and female figures carved of wood, argillite, and bone that generically portrayed the typical roles through which natives encountered non-Indians. Such figures, carved as curio articles, are an uncanny record of native perceptions of stereotypical European dress codes and attitudes. The figures of this group adroitly and poignantly express the rigid, officious, and pious attitudes of the white teacher (a), trader (b), and missionary (c); the native figure (d) apparently is an Indian in the service of a European.   T.N.

21
British Columbia, Haida(?)
Ceremonial Rattle, nineteenth century
Wood, black and red pigment, spruce root,
l. 9½ in. (24.2 cm)
Gift of Margaret Kimberly
22.3.1893

22
Arizona, Hopi, First Mesa, Hano Village
Bowl, c. 1900–1907
Terra-cotta with black and red pigment,
h. 2½ in. (6.4 cm), diam. 7¼ in. (18.5 cm)
Signed: Numpayo
Bequest of Frank C. and Clara G. Churchill
46.17.10111

21 The dominant feature of Northwest Coast art is a complex and dense system of iconography based on schematized, distorted, and transformed representations of animals. Some are derived from real animals of the natural habitat, and some are depictions of mythic and fantastic creatures; each is adopted for its specific attributes, which structure the human world in its relation to nature and the cosmos. In Northwest Coast art, including that of the Haida people, the rattle represents, both visually and conceptually, one of the most complex symbols. Rattles were used by shamans as a conduit to the supernatural and also by chiefs in ceremonial dances. Most rattles were characterized by composite animal forms in which the mythic raven figured prominently. This example, in its combination of bird and bear, represents a compositional and perhaps also iconographic variation of the classic raven rattle. The bird lacks the typical raven trait: the small box carried in its beak, which represents the "box of daylight" stolen by the trickster raven from the Chief of Heaven and delivered to the world of humans, until then steeped in darkness. The bird in this example may be a kingfisher, an oyster catcher, or a crane.   T.N.

22 This signed bowl was made by the potter-artist Nampeyo. It is a beautiful example of the revival of the prehistoric Hopi design style known as Sikyatki. Nampeyo was responsible for initiating this revival in the late nineteenth century, inspired by the Sikyatki prototypes then being discovered in archaeological excavations. Nampeyo's designs, like their prototypes, are characterized by intricate abstract motifs derived from animals. The central motif on this bowl may be read as representing bear paws and the peripheral motifs as rainbird beaks.   T.N.

23
New Mexico, Acoma Pueblo
Water Jar, c. 1900
Terra-cotta with pigment, h. 11 in. (27.9 cm),
diam. of neck 7½ in. (19.1 cm)
Bequest of Frank C. and Clara G. Churchill
46.17.10077

24
New Mexico, San Ildefonso Pueblo
Olla, c. 1890–1900
Terra-cotta with red, black, and white pigment,
h. 10¾ in. (27.4 cm), diam. of neck 7 in. (17.8 cm)
Bequest of Frank C. and Clara G. Churchill
46.17.10032

23 Made from a high-grade fine clay, Acoma pottery is renowned for its delicate but durable construction. Acoma potters generally treat the entire surface of the vessel as an open design field, using dense multiple patterns with some symmetry of juxtaposition. As in this example, the bottom is commonly delineated by a wide band of red slip. Flowers and birds are popular design elements, together with curvilinear abstract forms. A macaw parrot, also referred to as a rainbird, is represented here. Parrots lived in the wilds around this westernmost pueblo into the late nineteenth century and were revered as messengers of the sky—the source of rain.   T.N.

24 This water jar is a splendid example of traditional Pueblo pottery techniques, although it dates to the transitional phase between the end of the historic pottery period (1880) and the beginning of the modern period (c. 1900), when pottery was produced largely for a Euro-American clientele. The jar's well-defined shoulder and its polychrome decoration conform to the early works of San Ildefonso's famous potter-artist families such as the Martinez and the Montoyas.   T.N.

25
Alaska, Tlingit(?)
Pipe, nineteenth century
Walrus ivory, abalone shell,
copper lining, h. 4 in. (10.2 cm)
Gift of Mrs. James F. Scott in memory
of Victor Evans
157.9.13877

26
British Columbia, Haida(?)
Shaman's Charm, mid-nineteenth century
Bone, l. 8¼ in. (21.0 cm)
Gift of Margaret Kimberly
22.3.1919

27
British Columbia, Haida
Pipe, mid-nineteenth century
Argillite, l. 14½ in. (36.9 cm)
Gift of Margaret Kimberly
22.3.1905

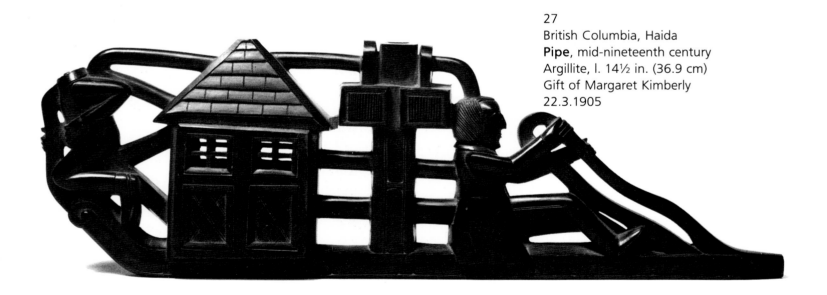

25 The use of tobacco as a stimulant was indigenous to many Native American cultures. The Tlingit and other peoples of the Northwest Coast sucked tobacco-and-lime pellets, but the custom of smoking was introduced by Russian seamen in Alaska during the late eighteenth century. Smoking subsequently became an adjunct to most ceremonial activities. The imagery of this fine example represents a hawk or thunderbird (above), a human face, and a bear (below). T.N.

26 Among the Haida and other native North Americans, the shaman, or medicine man, was the community's mediator with the world of supernatural forces. He was aided in his endeavor to invoke and control such forces by charms, typically in the form of animals endowed with symbolic significance. This charm, whose low-relief carving has retained the natural curve of the bone, represents a killer whale in profile. It was worn suspended horizontally from the shaman's neck or sewn onto his dance apron.   T.N.

27 Argillite, a Canadian carbonaceous shale, is a rare material found only on Queen Charlotte Island, home of the Haida. Native use of this black shale was rare before contact with white sailors, whalers, and traders intensified in the 1820s and 1830s, but argillite carving subsequently developed in response to a growing demand for curios on the part of this clientele. The early argillite sculptures, mostly in the form of pipes, portrayed traditional Haida animal imagery. But the Haida's fascination with the white man's world soon found expression in charmingly naïve portrayals of that world

28
Arizona, Pima
Storage Basket, 1907
Split cattail stems, black devil's-claw
(martynia), willow stitching,
h. 17¾ in. (45.1 cm)
Bequest of Frank C. and Clara G. Churchill
46.17.9452

(see number 20). Ships—important in the Haida's own island culture—became favorite themes. This example represents a steamship, perhaps a whaler, with the cabin, smokestack, rudder, figurehead (whose head is missing), and a helmsman. The elongated open-relief panel form, in which the smokestack contains the pipe bowl, defies our idea of a pipe. Indeed, this object of early-contact curio art was created for aesthetic appreciation and was not intended to be used.   T.N.

28 Baskets of this type, exhibiting the coiling technique used by the Pima but the form of a Southwestern water jar—atypical in traditional Pima basketry—appeared about 1900. They were made in response to the tastes of a growing tourist trade. This example was made by Melissa Jones of the village of Bapcha in 1907. It shows the fret motif traditionally employed by Pima basket weavers. Designs were usually executed in black (martynia) against the light background of willow stitches and are thought to be decorative rather than symbolic.   T.N.

29
Minnesota, Ojibway
Bandolier, c. 1900
Glass trade beads, cotton cloth
foundation and lining, silk trim,
h. 43 in. (109.2 cm)
Bequest of Frank C. and Clara G. Churchill
46.17.9872

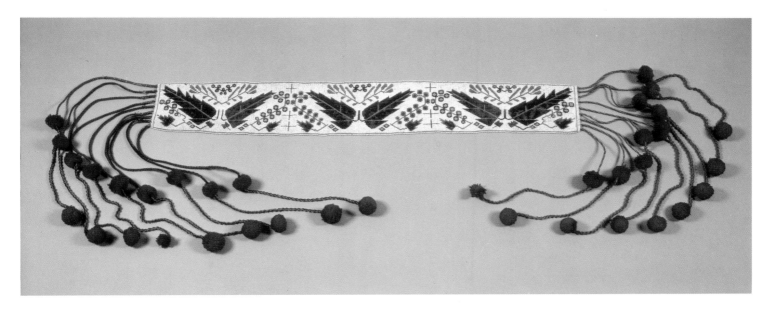

---

29 The bandolier derived from the plain carryall pouch first used by hunters and travelers. Probably modeled after the European shot pouch, it gradually changed in form and use to become a decorated accessory to formal male clothing. These shoulder bags were used by members of the Midewiwin society to contain personal and sacred articles during the society's closed ceremonies. In the latter part of the nineteenth century, the bandolier became a solely decorative element consisting of a flat panel, as in this example, rather than an actual bag. These were often worn in pairs, one over each shoulder. The bead design also evolved—from earlier stylized symmetrical patterns to the exuberant naturalistic and curvilinear floral representations evident here. The technique of beading is of the spot-stitch, or overlay, variety.   T.N.

30 As accessories of formal dress, belts of this type were often worn by men along with one or two bandoliers. The bead design of this belt is loom-woven rather than sewn to the surface, and this technique has determined the rectilinear nature of the pattern. Here, however, the inherent constraints of weaving in straight lines have been beautifully adapted to the organic shapes of leaf and flower forms.   T.N.

31 This bandolier has retained its pouch function (see number 29). Its bead design exhibits the rectilinear style characteristic of loom-woven beading (see number 30). The motif was influenced by the design of Oriental carpets brought west by white settlers. The harmonious soft-toned colors temper as well as integrate the density of the design.   T.N.

AFRICAN ART

UNTIL the modern era, African art was primarily in the domain of ethnography. It was housed and exhibited as part of the universal documentation of human cultures in ethnology and natural history museums, which have amassed thousands of African artifacts since the time of colonial penetration in the late nineteenth century. During the decades around 1900 serious aesthetic interest in African objects was sparked only sporadically, as for instance by the heralded discovery of Benin brass and bronze objects then considered exceptional among African works. It was the artistic avant-garde of the early twentieth century—particularly in France—that was instrumental in establishing African wood sculpture as worthy of lasting aesthetic acclaim. These artists—primary among them Picasso—were in the process of disavowing the traditional conventions of representation in nineteenth-century European painting and sculpture. They found in African "tribal" forms a mode of vital, charged expression that was congruent with their own search for a new meaning of art and its relationship to life. While these artists did not specifically consider the iconographic meanings of African sculpture, they did apprehend two crucial aspects of African art: the integration of content and significant form (the dimension that distinguishes true art from other expressions), and the visual expression of conceptual relationships *between* phenomena, rather than simple naturalistic imitation. The task of documenting and explicating these salient features of African art would be pursued by a later generation of ethnographers and art historians, who began work in the early 1960s.

During the decades between 1920 and 1950, ethnographers, colonial administrators, missionaries, and travelers continued to bring artifacts and art objects out of Africa, enriching the collections of museums. This period also saw the emergence of important private collections, particularly in Europe. Between the two world wars, private collectors and dealers were increasingly interested in the aesthetic qualities of African objects. Concurrent with this developing connoisseurship, the first publications of intellectual discourse on African art appeared. These addressed such central art-historical concerns as style analysis and classification, albeit in a tentative, if not speculative, manner. Exhibitions of African objects as art, distinct from ethnographic artifacts, began to be organized by private galleries, especially in France, and by museums. Historic exhibitions were held in New York by the Brooklyn Museum in 1923 ("Negro Art") and the Museum of Modern Art in 1935 ("African Negro Art"). This continuing engagement with African art on the part of a cultural elite in Europe and the United States culminated in the 1950s when African art emerged as one of the most exciting and provocative art forms. In the United States especially, it seemed an answer to the quest for a universal aesthetic within late Modernism (see, for example, number 135). African art thus resumed a role in the history of modern art.

Modern artists have continued to collect African art, and in many private collections African art is collected in tandem with modern art. At the same time, contextual documentation of its unique visual and cultural properties has accelerated since the 1950s due to the inclusion of African art within the discipline of art history. The growth of scholarship in the field of African art, combining the methods and interpretive perspectives of art history, ethnography, and archaeology, has been nothing short of spectacular.

The artistic traditions of Africa can now be appreciated in their full diversity. Wood, metal, and stone sculpture, fiber constructions, and terra-cotta and ivory objects have all been recognized as deserving of serious investigation, and their significance within their specific cultural ambients is being explored.

Most African artistic traditions developed in relatively small agrarian, pre-industrial communities throughout the black continent. Evidence for the earliest art traditions comes in the form of terracotta sculpture from Nigeria, where the Nok culture developed between 500 B.C. and A.D. 200. The dominant tradition of wood sculpture can be dated only to the nineteenth century, for in the extreme climatic conditions of Africa, the perishable medium of wood has little longevity. Nevertheless, one can assume a considerable age for the well-developed carving traditions of the nineteenth century; in rare cases such evidence exists—for example, in West Africa, where the Tellem culture is known to have produced wood sculpture between the thirteenth and fifteenth centuries.

Art as an artifact of culture partakes of the values, the ideas, and moral concepts that structure the *gestalt* of its society. African art, with its strong functional aspect, is solidly predicated on the various cultural systems from which it is generated. It is not an art-for-art's-sake phenomenon, but owes its existence to the need for maintaining the secular and spiritual order of society. This pragmatic aspect of art, now all but lost in our own society, does not preclude the subliminal and symbolic dimensions that characterize all art. These are not only abundant in African art, but indeed typify its integration of form and meaning. Forms, materials, and iconography are all based on symbolic systems that order human life in relation to the cosmos, the natural environment, and the human condition. Accordingly, we find representations of human and animal forms as statuary and masks that are imbued with conceptual references to the spirit world, the ancestors, fertility, magic, political authority, prestige, and social arbitration. The contexts in which figures and masks are used cover the full spectrum of ritual, ceremonial, and ordinary activities and are subject to culturally prescribed norms of behavior. Such norms often dictate the purposive presence of art objects in nonpublic contexts, accessible only to special-interest groups. The exceptions are certain public masquerades that are performed before an entire community.

African sculptors, always male and generally anonymous, deserve special mention. Their anonymity in Western art-historical terms does not reflect a lack of status or recognition. On the contrary, they were accorded honor and renown as well as material rewards in their own societies. They did not sign their works because they gave expression to collective rather than individual values. But a good carver was as known, acclaimed, and remembered within his own society as artists are in ours.

The African collection of the Hood Museum of Art is similar to those of other, larger museums in that it includes its share of ethnographic material. However, the focus of this handbook precludes the illustration of artifacts of primarily ethnographic interest. The African art objects included here reflect the Dartmouth collection, which attempts to document a broad range of types and styles from Africa's major art-producing areas. In the past, the primarily instructional purpose of the College Museum (see page 10) promoted breadth of representation over individual masterpieces. In recent years, however, Evelyn A. and William B. Jaffe have been an important force in strengthening the collection with their gifts of such works. The materialization of the Hood Museum of Art in the form of its new building provides a welcome opportunity to expand this mission and further strengthen the quality of the collection.   T.N.

32
Mali, Dogon
Vessel with Horse Head and Tail,
nineteenth to early twentieth century
Wood, l. 55 in. (139.7 cm)
Gift of John Friede, Class of 1960
Mis.968.79

33
RIGHT
Ivory Coast, Senufo, Korhogo area
Initiation Society Mask (Kpelie),
nineteenth century
Wood, h. 14¾ in. (37.5 cm)
Gift of Evelyn A. and William B. Jaffe,
Class of 1964H
S.972.15

34
FAR RIGHT
Mali, Bamana (Bambara)
Seated Female Figure,
nineteenth century
Wood with brass, h. 24 in. (61.0 cm)
Gift of Evelyn A. and William B. Jaffe,
Class of 1964H
S.972.10

32 This vessel may represent the ark of Dogon mythology in which a blacksmith, the Dogon culture hero, descended from sky to earth together with the first Dogon people. Containers such as this one are rare in Western collections. They may have been part of the ritual paraphernalia of Dogon priests, the Hogons, and may also have functioned as watering troughs for the Hogons' horses. A horse was considered an important status indicator of the priest's office.   T.N.

33 Typical of Senufo iconography, this mask is dominated by a double human face and a fully realized hornbill, one of the five primordial animals in Senufo mythology. Double-face masks allude to the male and female principles of the universe, represented here by male and female faces. The woman's face is characterized by the adornment of a lip plug. *Kpelie* masks were used by the male secret society known as Poro during the initiation of its members and at their funeral rites. These masks may also have been used in public entertainments outside the Poro context.   T.N.

34 This sculpture of a female figure with a transverse hair crest exhibits features associated with the northern, or Segou, style of the Bamana figurative repertoire: high bust; free, truncated arms; and solid, blocklike feet. Whether it functioned as an ancestral figure or an offertory receptacle has not been determined. This sculpture was one of the first African works to be recognized by Western connoisseurs as a masterpiece of African art. In 1935, when it was in the collection of the French painter Louis Marcoussis, this sculpture was included in the pioneer exhibition of African art held at the Museum of Modern Art, New York.   T.N.

35
BELOW
Mali, Bamana (Bambara), Ouassoulou area
Antelope Headdress (Chi Wara),
nineteenth to early twentieth century
Wood, h. 22 in. (56.0 cm)
Gift of Evelyn A. and
William B. Jaffe, Class of 1964H
S.972.3

37
Ivory Coast, Guro
Men's Secret Society Mask,
nineteenth century
Wood with traces of white and
red pigment, h. 16 in. (40.6 cm)
Gift of Evelyn A. and
William B. Jaffe, Class of 1964H
S.972.16

36
Guinea, Baga/Nalu
Serpent (Bansonyi),
early to mid-twentieth century
Wood with white, red, and black
pigment, h. 82 in. (208.3 cm)
Gift of Evelyn A. and
William B. Jaffe, Class of 1964H
S. 972.13

35 The antelope *chi wara*, "the beast who labors," is the mythic animal and culture hero who brought agriculture to the Bamana. This *chi wara* headdress is a characteristic example of the southwestern Bamana type in which a stylized roan antelope surmounts a similarly stylized anteater. *Chi wara* headdresses, representing either male or female antelopes, are attached to basketry caps and worn in public performances during young men's agricultural work, exhorting them to become champion cultivators and symbolically manifesting the importance of agriculture in Bamana life. T.N.

36 Attenuated representations of male and female serpents, *bansonyi*, are the primary symbolic agents of Simo, the male initiation society of the Baga people. *Bansonyi* preside over the Simo initiation camp, and their images are used as protective and creative devices. In this context they are believed to have the power to destroy witches and to cure sterility and illness. As neighboring ethnic groups in Guinea, the Baga and Nalu both produce serpent representations of this type. T.N.

37 Guro masks embody those qualities of an African aesthetic—stylized realism and delicacy of form and surface treatment—that appealed to early European and American collectors of African art. At the same time, the admiration of these masks exemplifies the gap between a well-developed connoisseurship of certain types of African art and a comprehension of their cultural context. With regard to masks such as this, the limited evidence available from the nineteenth century points to a function in the context of political authority and social control under the aegis of male secret societies. T.N.

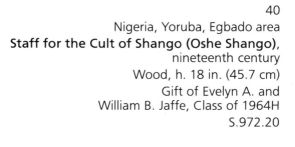

38
Nigeria, Yoruba, Oshogbo-Ilobu area
Dog Figure for the Cult of Shango,
nineteenth to early twentieth century
Wood, h. 19 in. (48.3 cm)
Gift of Evelyn A. and William B. Jaffe,
Class of 1964H
S. 972.19

40
Nigeria, Yoruba, Egbado area
Staff for the Cult of Shango (Oshe Shango),
nineteenth century
Wood, h. 18 in. (45.7 cm)
Gift of Evelyn A. and
William B. Jaffe, Class of 1964H
S.972.20

39
Nigeria, Yoruba,
probably Oyo Kingdom
Staff for the Cult of Eshu Elegba,
twentieth century
Wood and leather, h. 17 in. (43.2 cm)
Gift of Evelyn Jaffe Hall
S. 973.314

38 Shango shrine sculpture in the form of dogs apparently occurs only among the northeastern Yoruba. Such canine representations are rare in Western collections, and their meaning and function in relation to the deity Shango currently is not known. T.N.

39 Eshu, the mischievous orisha and symbol of uncertainty in Yoruba cosmology, is an embodiment of the age-old trickster figure. Among the Yoruba, his iconographic attributes include, as seen here, a hairdress in phallic form (*ogo Elegba*) and medicinal gourds (in the figure's right hand and in bands along the hairdress). A priest of Eshu wears such a staff hooked over the left shoulder, the hairdress providing the hook, just as one is worn by the figure represented in this staff. T.N.

40 Dance staffs such as this one are carried by priests and priestesses while they are possessed by the orisha Shango, god of thunder and lightning and symbol of life's vital, but ambivalent, forces. The head projection represents a double thunderbolt celt believed to be hurled upon earth by Shango when lightning flashes and thunder claps. The female figure depicts a Shango cult devotee in the kneeling posture of supplication. T.N.

41
Nigeria, Eastern Igbo or Middle Cross River
Janiform Mask,
nineteenth to early twentieth century
Wood with white and black pigment,
h. 17 in. (43.2 cm)
Purchase made possible through the
William B. and Evelyn A. Jaffe Fund
S.984.14

41 The two faces of this helmet mask are harmoniously integrated by three arched cranial projections that are analogous to the coiffures of the maiden spirit masks of the Western Igbo people. At the same time, the mask demonstrates visual and conceptual traits of the Igbo's Cross River neighbors. For instance, the concept of duality, represented here by male and female faces, is widespread among the peoples on both sides of the Cross River. This mask is an example, from the artistic realm, of the diffusion and exchange of cultural traits that characterize this complex culture area.   T.N.

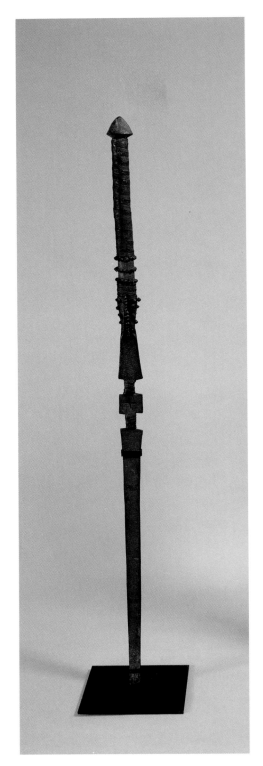

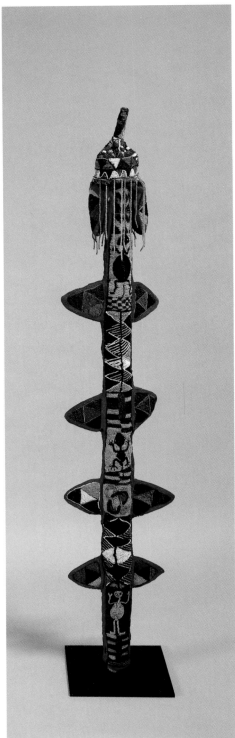

42

Nigeria, Yoruba

**Staff with Beaded Sheath and
Crown for the Cult of Orisha Oko,**
early to mid-twentieth century

Staff: iron, wood,
h. 56½ in. (143.5 cm)
Sheath: glass trade beads,
cloth foundation, hide,
h. 52 in. (132.1 cm)
Crown: glass trade beads, cloth
foundation over fiber frame,
h. 7 in. (17.8 cm)

Gift of Evelyn Jaffe Hall
S.973.322a–c

42 The staff, called *opa orisha Oko*, is a symbol of orisha Oko, whose name literally means "god of the farm." The devotees of this cult are women who appeal to the deity for the gift of fertility and for curative powers. Orisha Oko is said to have been the mythic king or queen of the northwestern Yoruba village of Irawo, whose blacksmiths produce the iron staffs that are used in the cult throughout Yoruba lands. In accord with orisha Oko's royal status, the staff, when not in use, may be sheathed by elaborate bead-work, the prerogative of Yoruba royalty. The beaded sheath, *ewu orisha Oko* (*ewu* means clothed), may be further enhanced by a small beaded crown, a miniature version of the crown worn by Yoruba kings, perched atop the sheath.   T.N.

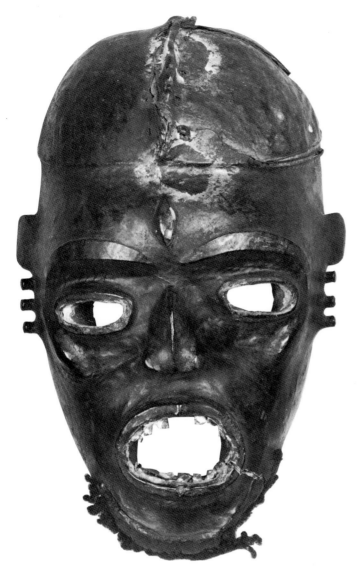

44
Cameroon, Western Grassfields
Mask of Authority, c. 1900
Wood with camwood powder and kaolin,
h. 21½ in. (54.6 cm)
Purchase through the William B. and Evelyn A. Jaffe Fund
S.973.164

43
Cameroon, Widekum
Men's Secret Society Mask (Agwe Chaka),
twentieth century
Wood covered with antelope hide, raffia palm
bark (teeth), hair, kaolin, h. 17 in. (43.2 cm)
Gift of Evelyn Jaffe Hall
S.973.318

43 This domed mask of almost skull-like appearance is related in type to the skin-covered helmet masks and head crests from the Upper and Middle Cross River culture zones. It was used by the Widekum in memorial funerary celebrations for members of the Nchiba warriors' society. The glistening patina of the skin, resulting from repeated applications of palm oil, as well as traces of kaolin around the eye sockets and mouth—both usually applied before a masquerade performance—attest to the use of this mask.   T.N.

44 In the Cameroon Grassfields, a culture area typified by sociopolitical stratification, the ownership of masks is vested in the palace and elite groups of male titleholders and is indicative of social prestige and attendant economic privileges. In secret and public appearances, masks facilitate and legitimize the exercise of power through their time-honored symbols of the community's primary beliefs and values. Such symbols, invested with the collective authority of culture, are recognized and understood by the community, and they persistently reaffirm the established order of society—an order perceived as decreed by successive generations of ancestors and therefore unquestionable. The male face and prestigious headdress (worn by kings and high titleholders), as seen in this mask, are symbolic of the governance and wisdom of male authority. Together they form one of the standard icons in the art of the Cameroon Grassfields.   T.N.

45
Zaire, Suku
Initiation Mask (Hemba),
nineteenth to early twentieth century
Wood with traces of red
and white pigment,
h. 17 in. (43.2 cm)
Gift of Evelyn A. and
William B. Jaffe,
Class of 1964H
S.972.8

46
Gabon, Tsogo
Half-figure for a Reliquary,
early twentieth century
Wood, hide, brass, cotton cloth,
traces of black and red pigment,
h. 14½ in. (36.9 cm)
Gift of Evelyn A. and
William B. Jaffe, Class of 1964H
S.967.122

45 This fine example of a Suku *hemba* mask is distinguished by the delicate articulation of its features, such as the incised markings of the hairdress, and by the grace and strength of the surmounting antelope, which is compositionally integrated with the domed cranium of the mask helmet. The antelope is symbolic of speed and agility—significant qualities in a culture where hunting is an important subsistence pursuit. Thus the mask's appearance during rites of initiation into social manhood poignantly restates a central value in Suku culture.   T.N.

46 This figure, from the Tsogo people, illustrates the tradition of ancestor worship among cultures of the Ogowe River Basin, a tradition that has spawned the well-known guardian figures of the Fang and Kota people. This figure would have been set into a receptacle, the reliquary, containing ancestral bones and accoutrements, including jewelry. The projecting half-figure guarded the revered ancestral remains with a forbidding stare, which is effected by prominent disk eyes of brass and iron that were kept gleaming.   T.N.

47 Fetish figures are common in the art of central Africa. They usually consist of wood to which various human-made and natural substances have been added. These substances are perceived as having potent properties—either inherently or through activation by a specialist—that can be channeled toward benevolent or malevolent purposes. The fetish thus can function either as a protective and curative, or an aggressive and destructive, device.

47
Zaire, Teke
Fetish Figure, twentieth century
Wood with glass, h. 13⅞ in. (35.0 cm)
Gift of Evelyn A. and William B. Jaffe,
Class of 1964H
S.972.7

48
Zaire, Lulua
**Protective Female Figure for
Warriors**(?), twentieth century
Wood with white and red pigment,
h. 24 in. (61.0 cm)
Gift of Evelyn A. and
William B. Jaffe, Class of 1964H
S.972.104

Among the Teke, the torsos of fetish figures such as this one—known as *butti*—are typically composed of an aggregate of potent substances held together by a resinous coating or cloth and forming an articulated globe around the body's trunk. In this example a globe is approximated, but atypically it is carved of solid wood with a mirror glass as the only added element. Mirror fetishes are common among the Kongo, western neighbors of the Teke, and this example may represent an assimilation of the use of a mirror. Apart from that, the figure shows typical Teke traits: vertical facial scarification, a beard, and a hairdress with a prominent central crest. The functions of this type of fetish figure among the Teke are reported to be the promotion of health, family relationships, trade, and success in hunting.   T.N.

48 Most Lulua statuary displays delicate modeling of body forms and rich curvilinear surface ornamentation. This male figure does not conform to that aesthetic norm. It shares the iconographic features typical of larger Lulua male figures—the hairdress with a central point, the accentuated navel as focus of the torso, the loincloth simulating a leopard skin, neck ornamentation representing prestigious bead necklaces, and the profusion of patterned scarification—but the rendering of these features lacks the subtlety and almost rococo ornateness for which Lulua sculpture is known. While the statue is a genuine Lulua work, it may be of recent origin.   T.N.

49
Zaire, Luba
Stool for a Chief, twentieth century
Wood, h. 17¼ in. (43.8 cm)
William B. and Evelyn A. Jaffe Fund
S.972.189

50
Zaire, Mbagani
Initiation Mask, twentieth century
Wood with white and red pigment,
h. 13½ in. (34.3 cm)
Gift of John Friede, Class of 1960
S.968.76

49 The custom of dignifying a chief through exclusive use of a stool, whose seat is symbolically supported by a human figure, is found in several cultures of Africa. Primary among these are the people of the Cameroon Grassfields and the Luba, Songe, and Chokwe of central Africa. Among the matrilineal Luba, the caryatid predominates. Its scarification patterns are those of high-ranking women of royal lineage. These composed and serene female stool-figures,

often rendered with uplifted arms that support the stool's platform, may be interpreted as representing the chief's royal female ancestors. As such they are symbols of the essential feature of Luba social organization and the continuity of the royal dynasty.

In its style, this stool exhibits typical Luba Shankandi traits, such as the fluent, rounded lines of the torso, the serpentine legs, the squared chin, the pursed mouth, and the elongated oval eyes. The caryatid apparently was decorated in a pattern of brass studs, an unusual feature for a Luba caryatid stool.
T.N.

50 This face mask is of a rare type attributed to the Mbagani, a small and little-known group from central Africa. Its striking and expressive sculptural quality results from the dominance and positioning of the over-articulated eye sockets, which simulate the simultaneous perception of the mask's profile and front. Beyond scant references to male circumcision and initiation rites, nothing is known of the meaning of this mask type.
T.N.

EUROPEAN ART

CHARACTERISTIC of Dartmouth's early collections, the first European works of art to be accessioned were portraits. In 1829 William Legge, the fourth earl of Dartmouth, presented the college library with a portrait of his grandfather by the English painter Samuel Reynolds. This portrait is a copy of a painting by Sir Joshua Reynolds formerly in the Foundling Hospital, London. A pair of portraits representing an English Restoration courtier and his lady by a seventeenth-century Flemish artist were given by the artist-alumnus Albert Hoit in 1842. These joined numerous American works, which had been donated by alumni or commissioned by the college, on display in Dartmouth's Gallery of Paintings.

In 1880 *Simeon and the Infant Savior*, a painting attributed to Jusepe Ribera, was given to the college by Mrs. J. C. Bodwell. Fourteen years later, a significant group of nineteen Greek icons was purchased for the college through George Dana Lord, professor of archaeology, while he was on a class trip to Greece. In addition to those reproduced here (numbers 51 and 52), noteworthy examples include *St. John on Patmos*, an icon of the mid-seventeenth century, and a sixteenth-century panel, *Virgin and Child in the Fountain of Life*. The museum's collection of icons was increased again in 1959 by ten Russian works from the Ralph S. Bartlett bequest.

By the early twentieth century, holdings of European art, particularly in the area of prints and drawings, began to expand more rapidly. Purchases were made possible through the Guernsey Center Moore Fund, the Julia L. Whittier Fund, and by donations from Professor George Breed Zug. These acquisitions formed the core of a collection of graphic art that has continued to grow thanks to gifts from generous donors too numerous to name individually. Special mention should be made, however, of George Abrams, Mrs. Hersey Egginton, Ilse Bischoff, Mr. and Mrs. William B. Jaffe, Mr. and Mrs. M. R. Schweitzer, Mr. and Mrs. Ivan Albright, Daisy Shapiro, Fredrick Hirschland, Helena M. Wade, and Philip Hofer. Recently, the fund established by the class of 1935 has enabled the museum to further enrich its holdings of graphic art. Highlights of the collection of works on paper include watercolors by Auguste Rodin, Paul Signac, André Derain, Stuart Davis, and Arthur Dove; drawings by Maerten van Heemskerck, Giovanni Battista Piranesi, Benjamin West, Jean-François Millet, Edgar Degas, Mary Cassatt, Amedeo Modigliani, Charles Burchfield, and Maximilien Luce; and a collection of some 9,000 prints and posters.

The museum has also depended on the generosity of donors to expand the collection of European paintings, sculpture, and decorative arts. When Carpenter Hall was built in 1929 to house the art department, Robert Jackson, class of 1900, contributed a magnificent sixteenth-century mantelpiece from the château of François I at Chenonceaux. In the 1930s Mrs. Moses Dyer Carbee donated Pieter Jacob Horemans's *Still Life* and a Dutch-inspired *Village Scene* attributed to the Italian painter Antonio Amorosi, among other works. In this area, as in so many others, Mr. and Mrs. William B. Jaffe have played a significant role. Their contributions to the museum's European holdings began with the donation of Edouard Vuillard's *Seascape at Honfleur* (number 82) in 1954 and over the years have included bronze putti by Nicolò Roccatagliata and Ercole Ferrata, a seventeenth-century sculpture of St. John the Evangelist attributed to the German Master of Pürten, an Impressionist work entitled *In the Garden* attributed to Berthe Morisot, and more than fifty Spanish drawings (see number 63).

During the 1950s, thanks to the interest of numerous art patrons and donors, the museum was strengthened in the areas of Flemish and Dutch Baroque painting, a trend that attests to the popularity of these styles among American collectors. Through gifts from Paul W. Doll and Mr. and Mrs. Jesse D. Wolff, Ludolf Backhuyzen's *Harbor Scene with Warships* and Roelof Jansz. de Vries's *Landscape with Ruins* were added to the northern European works in the collection.

Julia and Richard H. Rush, class of 1937, have contributed significantly to the range and quality of the museum's holdings, particularly in the art of the Baroque period. Beginning with a gift in 1958 of the large Flemish painting *Jason and the Golden Fleece* (number 72), and including Cornelius Johnson's *Portrait of an English Gentleman* (number 61), Pieter van Laer's *Street Scene with Mora Players* (number 66), Johannes Voorhout's *Good Samaritan*, in addition to Italian paintings by Luca Giordano (number 70), Marco Palmezzano (number 59), Pietro da Cortona, Luca Cambiaso, and, more recently, Bernardo Strozzi's *Berenice*, the Rushes have been among the most important donors to the art collection of Dartmouth College. Their gift of two portraits by the English painter George

Romney (see number 73) has expanded the museum's portrait holdings, an emphasis that has been a forte of the collection since its inception.

In the area of French nineteenth-century painting and sculpture, Mr. and Mrs. M. R. Schweitzer's contributions have been of primary importance. With their first donation in 1959, of a bronze sculpture, *Portrait of Paul Cézanne*, executed by Richard Guino under the direction of Auguste Renoir, and including the gifts in 1964 of *Salome* by Jean-Jacques Henner and *Lion with a Gilded Mane* by Antoine-Louis Barye, the Schweitzers have assumed a significant role in shaping the current collection of European works. Their donations have also enhanced the museum's group of eighteenth-century genre paintings—with *Peasant Interior* by Michel Lépicié and *Young Girl with a Straw Hat* by William Owen—and European landscapes—with Emile Bernard's *Landscape, Aix-les-Bains* and Félix Vallotton's *Landscape with Shepherd Boy*. Additional gifts have extended the portrait collection into the areas of sixteenth-century Italy, with *Portrait of a Lady as Astronomy* (number 60) attributed to Lavinia Fontana, and mid-nineteenth-century France, with Charles Chaplin's *Portrait of a Young Girl*. Nineteenth-century academic history painting is represented by another Schweitzer gift, a large *Hagar and Ishmael in the Wilderness* by Johann Ender.

More recently, the artist Ivan Albright and his wife, Josephine Patterson Albright, donated important works of European art. *Woman at Her Toilette* by Paul Cézanne (number 83), a watercolor of a nude by Georges Braque, and *Girls at a Flower Fair, Dieppe* by Camille Pissarro (number 81) have strengthened the collection of French watercolors from the late nineteenth and early twentieth centuries.

Though not the strongest area of the Dartmouth College collection, European art is represented at the Hood Museum by an especially fine group of prints and an interesting and varied collection of paintings, drawings, and watercolors.

The European holdings continue to grow with recent purchases selected to enhance the areas of Dutch genre painting—with Cornelius Saftleven's *Barn Interior* (number 65)—and French nineteenth-century academic painting—with Ernest Leroux's *Woman Holding up a Child to Aesculapius*.　P.F.

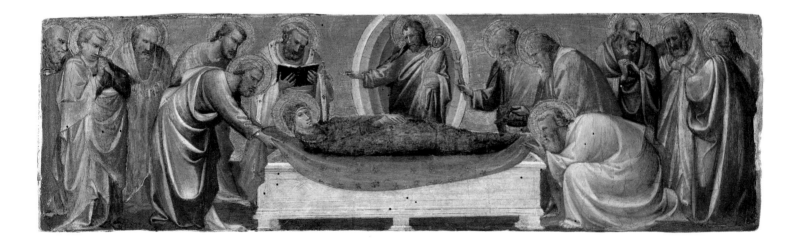

51 Large icons of this type were used in the decoration of Byzantine churches, combined in screens and placed about the altar or hung in tiers along the walls and pillars. Befitting its function, the panel depicts three of the five Fathers of the Greek Church, identified by their liturgical garments and by the inscription of their names in the gold ground. Absent are St. Athanasius and St. Cyril.   P.F.

52 Adherence to tradition was a key factor in the creation of Byzantine-style religious icons, even long after the end of the Byzantine Empire. Since icons functioned primarily as spiritual objects, their style, symbolism, and iconography, once established, changed slowly. This *Annunciation*, for example, has innumerable relatives in Greek, Russian, and Cypriote churches and museums, ranging in date from the thirteenth to the seventeenth century. Two versions, however, are nearly identical to the Dartmouth panel: one, a Greek *Annunciation* in the Benaki Museum, Athens, is dated 1585; another, of Cypriote

origin, has been dated to 1540. Such evidence suggests that this icon probably was produced in the mid-sixteenth century. Other aspects of the work—the grace of the figures, the quality of coloring, and the relative accuracy of perspective in the architectural details—reveal the individual touches of an especially skilled craftsman. P.F.

51
FAR LEFT
Greek, seventeenth century
Three Church Fathers
Oil on canvas on wood, 46½ × 40¼ in. (118.2 × 102.3 cm)
Inscribed, upper left: *Ho Hagios Basilios* [St. Basil];
upper center: *Ho Hagios Iō[annēs] Chrisostomos* [St. John Chrysostom];
upper right: *Ho Hagios Grigorios ho Theologos*
[St. Gregory the Theologian]
Purchase through Professor George Dana Lord, Class of 1884
P.894.7

52
LEFT
Greek, sixteenth century
The Annunciation, c. 1540–85
Tempera on canvas on wood, 18¼ × 14⅜ in. (46.4 × 36.4 cm)
Inscribed upper center: *Ho Euangelēsmos* [The Annunciation];
upper left: *Ho Arch[angelos] Ga[b]riēl* [Archangel Gabriel];
upper right: *M[atē]r Th[eo]u* [Mother of God]
Purchase through Professor George Dana Lord, Class of 1884
P.894.25

53
BELOW LEFT
Master of the Bambino Vispo (probably
Gherardo Starnina, Italian, c. 1354–c. 1413)
Death of the Virgin, c. 1405–10
Tempera on panel with tooled gold leaf,
7 × 22¼ in. (17.8 × 56.5 cm)
Gift of Mr. and Mrs. Ray Winfield Smith,
Class of 1918
P.975.5

54
French, Burgundy, fifteenth century
St. Barbara, c. 1470–90
Polychromed wood, h. 37½ in. (95.2 cm)
Gift of John Philip Kassebaum
and Edward A. Hansen
S.981.102

---

53 This small panel, representing the death of the Virgin, formed part of a predella, the lower section of an altarpiece. On the basis of its style it has been attributed with some certainty to the Master of the Bambino Vispo. This artist's precise identity is not known, but his characteristic portrayal of an especially lively (*vispo*) Christ Child in other paintings has enabled scholars to identify works by his hand and has given him his designation. In a recent study Jeanne van Waadenoijen has presented convincing evidence that this unknown master may have been Gherardo Starnina, a Tuscan painter who worked in Valencia and possibly France and who played a decisive role in the spread of the International Gothic style to Florence. P.F.

54 This figure of St. Barbara, with its embroidered surcoat, pleated gown, and long cloak that falls in soft folds at the hem, is an adaptation of the famous version in the Musée Rolin, Autun. The type became popular in Burgundy in the fifteenth century, although it was traditionally executed in limestone. This version is rare in its use of the medium of polychromed wood. The realistic style made possible by this technique was popular with a growing middle-class audience in northern Europe during the late Middle Ages. P.F.

55

Martin Schongauer, German, c. 1450–1491
The Flagellation (number four from the
Passion series), c. 1475–80
Engraving, 6½ × 4½ in. (16.3 × 11.6 cm)
Signed in plate, lower center:
M + S [monogram]
Gift of Helena M. Wade in memory of
her husband, Alfred Byers Wade
Pr.950.21.41

Albrecht Dürer, German, 1471–1528
The Four Horsemen of the Apocalypse
(number three from the *Apocalypse*), c. 1497–98
Woodcut, prepublication proof,
15½ × 11 in. (39.4 × 28.1 cm)
Signed in block, lower center: *AD* [monogram]
Gift of Helena M. Wade in memory of her husband,
Alfred Byers Wade
Pr.950.21.10

---

55 The art of printing from engraved metal had its origins in German goldsmiths' shops toward the middle of the fifteenth century. These artisans found that they could better visualize the progress of their design by rubbing ink into the incised lines and then pressing dampened paper onto the engraved metal. The reproductive potential of this process was recognized almost immediately. Martin Schongauer seems to have been the first engraver who was primarily a painter rather than a goldsmith, and it is not a

coincidence that he is also the first engraver whose full name is known to us. Unlike paintings, prints travel easily, and the delicate grace of Schongauer's engravings had a great influence on other artists.   J.B.

56 Albrecht Dürer produced some of the most superb prints ever made. The son of a goldsmith, the young Dürer learned early the art of engraving. It was the humbler medium of woodcut, however, that Dürer raised to a level that has seldom been equaled. He was both artist and publisher for his *Apocalypse*, the appearance of which in 1498 was related

to the widespread belief that the end of the world would occur in 1500. Both the German and the Latin editions were printed so that each of the fourteen full-page woodcuts commanded the right-hand side of a double-page spread. *The Four Horsemen of the Apocalypse* is the most famous of the series. The Dartmouth impression has no text on the verso, indicating that it is a prepublication proof.   J.B.

57

Hendrik Goltzius, Dutch, 1558–1616
The Great Hercules, 1589
Engraving, second state of two, 22 × 16 in. (55.9 × 40.6 cm)
Signed and dated in plate, lower left: *HGoltzius Inuent. et Sculpt. Ao. 1589*;
inscribed in plate with the name of the publisher,
lower right: *ICVisscher excu.*
Acquisition Fund
Pr. 975.59

58

Hans Bol, Dutch, 1534–1593
Landscape with Hunters, c. 1575
Pen and bistre on paper,
7 × 10½ in. (17.8 × 26.7 cm)
Gift of Mrs. Hersey Egginton in
memory of her son, Everett,
Class of 1921
D.954.20.644

57 Hendrik Goltzius was a flamboyant artistic personality who took naturally to the Mannerist style, which was infiltrating his native Netherlands during the last quarter of the sixteenth century. That Goltzius was a virtuoso engraver is evident in this print, which has always been one of the artist's most popular works. Its size alone indicates a remarkable technical achievement, for it would have been extremely difficult, with the presses of the period, to print evenly from a copperplate this large. The grotesquely muscular Hercules seems a willful rebuke to the classical ideal of the Renaissance. This engraving may in fact be linked to the establishment of a chair for anatomy at the University of Leiden in 1589, the same year this print was executed. According to one account, the print was used in the Theatrum Anatomicum of the university as a demonstration piece.   J.B.

58 Best known for drawings and etchings of delicate figures set in wooded landscapes, Hans Bol presents in this sketch an excellent example of his mature style. Heavily influenced by Pieter Brueghel the Elder in his earliest works, Bol by the mid-1560s had abandoned the low horizon and religious themes of that style, replacing them with busy panoramic views characteristic of Mannerism in Antwerp in the late 1560s and early 1570s. In the mid-1570s Bol's style shifted once again, this time to the landscape type that would dominate his work until his death. Our drawing is typical of his work in that genre: small figures beside a large tree open the composition on the left; the viewer is led on a meandering path through an active middle ground of hills and a river valley; and the path terminates in an atmospheric distance near the center of the composition.   P.F.

59 *Madonna and Child with Saints Sebastian and Roch* resembles another altarpiece by Marco Palmezzano, *Madonna and Child with Saints John the Evangelist and Catherine of Alexandria* in the church of San Mercuriale, Forlì. As in our painting, Palmezzano signed that panel on a scrap of paper depicted at the lower edge of the marble flooring. Also similar are the architectural details of the Virgin's throne and the background landscape on the upper right. Since the San Mercuriale panel has been dated to about 1497, the Dartmouth altarpiece may have been painted in approximately the same period.   P.F.

60
Attributed to Lavinia Fontana, Italian, 1552–1614
Portrait of a Lady as Astronomy, c. 1585
Oil on canvas, 45⅛ × 36⅞ in. (114.6 × 93.7 cm)
Gift of Mr. and Mrs. M. R. Schweitzer
P.961.255

59
Marco Palmezzano, Italian, c. 1458–1539
**Madonna and Child with Saints Sebastian
and Roch,** c. 1497
Tempera on wood,
67 × 62¾ in. (170.3 × 159.4 cm)
Signed lower center: *[Ma]rcus Pa[l]mezo.*
Gift of Julia and Richard H. Rush,
Class of 1937
P.972.223

61
Cornelius Johnson (Cornelis Janssens van Ceulen),
English, 1593–c. 1664
Portrait of an English Gentleman, 1620
Oil on panel, 26¾ × 20 in. (67.9 × 50.8 cm)
Signed and dated lower right:
Co. Johnsono. fecit. 1620
Gift of Julia and Richard H. Rush, Class of 1937
P.962.132

60 This portrait of a woman recently has been attributed to Lavinia Fontana by Eleanor Tufts. Although the sitter has not been identified, she undoubtedly was a woman of high social standing, a conclusion suggested by her rich costume and jewelry. While women of the period traditionally were depicted with attributes such as a lap dog, symbolizing faithfulness, or a book, she is portrayed with her right hand on an armillary sphere. This instrument, which represents the principal circles of the heavens, is an attribute of astronomy, one of the seven liberal arts. Its inclusion in the portrait with the accompanying inscription SIC ARDVA (thus hardship), perhaps an abbreviated form of the motto "from hardship to the stars," may denote the subject's role as a woman of learning or as a personification of the learned science.   P.F.

61 Born in London of Dutch parents, Cornelius Johnson is considered to be among the finest English portraitists of the early seventeenth century. He was equally regarded in his own day, having been named court painter in 1632. Anticipating the outbreak of civil war in England, he left in 1643 for Holland, where he worked until his death. Our portrait is signed with the English form of the artist's name and dated 1620. The feigned oval surround, which attests to Johnson's artistic heritage in the miniature tradition, is characteristic of the artist's style during the 1620s, as are the type of landed gentleman depicted and the sensitive portrayal of the sitter's character through his physiognomy.   P.F.

62
Rembrandt Harmensz. van Rijn, Dutch, 1606–1669
The Angel Departing from the Family of Tobias, 1641
Etching, third state of four, 4 × 6 in. (10.3 × 15.4 cm)
Signed and dated in plate, lower left: *Rembrandt 1641*
Gift of Mrs. Hersey Egginton in memory of her son,
Everett, Class of 1921
Pr.954.20.684

63
Juan de Valdés Leal, Spanish, 1622–1690
St. Jerome in the Wilderness, 1684
Ink and wash on paper, 8⅝ × 6½ in. (22.0 × 16.5 cm)
Signed and dated lower left: *Baldes fe. ano 1684;*
inscribed lower right: *30 des Brit*[?]
Gift of Evelyn A. and William B. Jaffe, Class of 1964H
D.961.221.4

62 Like Martin Schongauer and Albrecht Dürer, Rembrandt van Rijn was as important a printmaker as he was a painter. Rembrandt's sensitivity to the realities of human emotion and his affection for humankind in general were conveyed particularly well in his etchings. The fresh, unpretentious quality of many of Rembrandt's etchings is exemplified by this little work. There is a spirit here not only of the reverence of this mystical moment but of humor as well. Among the principal figures, all eyes are decorously lowered as the departing angel makes a somewhat graceless exit to the upper right. J.B.

63 This drawing of *St. Jerome in the Wilderness*, signed "Baldes," was undoubtedly produced by the Spanish Baroque artist Juan de Valdés Leal, who at times used the phonetic spelling of his name as a signature. The expressive and virtuosic handling of the brush, as well as the theme of St. Jerome—one that recurs in this artist's oeuvre—further point to the drawing's creator as Juan de Valdés Leal rather than his son, Lucas (1661–1724), to whom the work also has been attributed.   P.F.

64

Giovanni Battista Piranesi, Italian, 1720–1778

Gallery with Arches and a Group of Prisoners (plate ten from *Invenzioni capric. di carceri*, 1752 edition), c. 1745–50

Etching, first state, 16⅛ × 21⅛ in. (41.0 × 53.6 cm)

Signed in plate, lower left: *Piranesi f.*; watermark: fleur-de-lis in circle

Transfer from the Sherman Art Library, Dartmouth College

Pr.977.25.60

64 The great eighteenth-century Italian architect and draftsman Giovanni Battista Piranesi was a prolific etcher, producing over one thousand prints in the course of his career. Dartmouth owns examples of almost one-quarter of the artist's etchings. Piranesi's fabulous series *Capricious Inventions of Prisons* was an early manifestation of the Romantic movement in Europe. Though at the time they were published the *Prisons* were far less popular than Piranesi's architectural and topographical prints, they are today his most famous works. These large etchings were published in several editions. The plates of the first edition, published about 1750, were lightly etched, and the resulting prints are relatively bright in tonality. Around 1761 Piranesi reworked the plates and added two additional compositions. In contrast to the first edition, the mood of this later edition is darker and more brooding. Dartmouth's rare set of the *Prisons* is from an intermediate edition of 1752 in which the plates were published by Bouchard as part of a portfolio of Piranesi's early work, the *Magnificenze di Roma*.   J.B.

65
Cornelius Saftleven, Dutch, 1607—1681
Barn Interior, c. 1665
Oil on panel, 23½ × 26⅜ in. (59.7 × 67.0 cm)
Signed lower left: *CS*
Julia L. Whittier and William S. Rubin Funds
P.983.10

66
Pieter van Laer, Dutch, 1592/95—c. 1642
Street Scene with Mora Players, c. 1625—38
Oil on canvas, 18½ × 15⅞ in. (47.0 × 40.2 cm)
Gift of Julia and Richard H. Rush, Class of 1937
P.962.153

65 A Dutch genre and landscape painter, Cornelius Saftleven played a key role in introducing the theme of the stable interior to genre painting. As is characteristic of many seventeenth-century Dutch works, this apparently secular subject nevertheless conveyed a moral message. The struggle between the cat and dog recalls expressions admonishing neglect, such as, "Dogs and cats like nothing better than reckless servants"; the servants, embracing on the stairway at the left, look out undaunted at the viewer and grin, suggesting another adage warning of the immorality of amorous grappling.   P.F.

66 This painting represents a type of genre subject that Pieter van Laer, known as Bamboccio, popularized during his stay in Rome (1625 to about 1638): *bambocciate*, naturalistic street scenes depicting peddlers, beggars, and card players. A soft lighting, which comes from a source outside the picture at the left and silhouettes the foreground figures against a dark middle ground, reveals the impact of the Roman experience on van Laer's style. The geometric simplicity of both figures and architecture foreshadows works by the American painter George Caleb Bingham, whose interest in artists like van Laer attests to the popularity of Dutch genre painting in America during the mid-nineteenth century.   P.F.

67
Francisco de Goya y Lucientes, Spanish, 1746–1828
Little Bulls' Folly (Disparate de Toritos), 1816–23
Etching, aquatint, and drypoint, trial proof,
8¼ × 12¾ in. (21.1 × 32.4 cm)
Gift of Philip Hofer
Pr.940.13

67 The tragic period of European history
spanned by Francisco de Goya's long life
found in him an eloquent witness. Goya's
most forceful print series is his *Disasters of
War*; Dartmouth has a number of examples
from the first edition, which was not published until after the artist's death. This
whimsical etching, *Little Bulls' Folly*, shows
another side of Goya's talent. It combines
two of his favorite subjects—the foolishness
of humankind and the bullring as a metaphor for life—into a marvelous work in
which wild-eyed little bulls tumble improba-
bly through space.   J.B.

68
Eugène Delacroix,
French, 1798–1863
**Study for a
Crucifixion Scene,** 1835
Pen and ink wash on paper,
8⅝ × 6 in. (21.9 × 15.3 cm)
Signed lower left: *E.D.*
Bertram Geller Memorial Fund
D.962.109

69
Thomas Couture,
French, 1815–1879
Portrait of a Gentleman,
1864
Black and white chalk
on blue paper,
21⅞ × 17 in.
(55.5 × 43.1 cm)
Signed and dated
lower right: *T.C. / 1864*
Julia L. Whittier Fund
D.967.99

68 Although this drawing by Eugène De-lacroix is documented as a study for his painting *Christ on the Cross between Two Thieves* of 1835 (Musée Municipal des Beaux-Arts, Vannes), it may also have served as a model for his *Crucifixion* of 1846, a painting now in the Walters Art Gallery, Baltimore. The composition of the Dart-mouth drawing reverses the figures of Christ and the Virgin in the earlier painting; how-ever, the crucified Christ is nearly identical to that of the later version. In addition, the figure at the lower right of our drawing finds his place, although reversed, in the left corner of the Baltimore *Crucifixion*.   P.F.

69 Characteristic of Thomas Couture's portraits of the 1850s and 1860s, this drawing presents a three-quarter view of the sitter with the greatest attention lavished on details of physiognomy. Given the degree of finish in its execution, as well as the presence of a signature and date, the drawing probably was considered a finished work rather than a preparatory study for a painting. Many of Couture's portraits of the 1860s were studies of his students done as demonstration pieces; this sketch may represent one such work. A faithful disciple described his teacher's working method as follows: "First, with a sharply-pointed charcoal he draws lightly a few delicate outlines that already suggest the portrait; then with bitumen, vermilion and cobalt, he puts in the thinnest, lightest *frotté*, drawing with absolute correctness every touch. He worked for two hours, sometimes exclaiming: 'Ah! how delicate it is! how difficult! . . . You see,' he said, 'that your professor does not paint with a *grand coup*, but with exceeding carefulness.'" It has been suggested that our drawing portrays the painter Frédéric Bazille (1841–1870), but Couture's sitter appears to be older than Bazille's twenty-three years in 1864. P.F.

70
Luca Giordano, Italian, 1632–1705
The Martyrdom of St. Lawrence, c. 1696
Oil on canvas, 60½ × 79¼ in. (153.6 × 201.3 cm)
Gift of Julia and Richard H. Rush, Class of 1937
P.971.32

70 A Neapolitan painter who studied first with his father, Antonio, and later with Jusepe Ribera, Luca Giordano developed a dramatic Baroque style that synthesized his knowledge of such masters as Pietro da Cortona, Paolo Veronese, and Mattia Preti. Nicknamed "Fa Presto," Giordano was renowned for his prodigious speed of execution. This example of Giordano's work is

unusual in its oval shape, a format that may be the result of later trimming. Although undated, our painting is related to another *Martyrdom of St. Lawrence* by Giordano in the Escorial, Madrid, which is dated 1696. P.F.

71 Executed in the style of Caravaggio, with sharp contrasts of light and dark and a hand illusionistically breaking into the viewer's space, this painting of *St. Paul the Hermit and the Raven* has been attributed to Giacinto Brandi. Born in Poli, a small town near Rome, Brandi traveled to Naples, where he studied with Giovanni Lanfranco and Jusepe Ribera. In its strong chiaroscuro and the features of the aging saint, this painting is remarkably similar to another work by Brandi, *A Saint Reading*, now at the Smith College Museum of Art, Northampton, Mas-

71
Attributed to Giacinto Brandi, Italian, 1623–1691
St. Paul the Hermit and the Raven, c. 1665
Oil on canvas, 38 × 28¾ in. (96.5 × 73.0 cm)
Bequest of Martin F. Huberth, Jr., Class of 1925
P.976.12

72
Studio of Peter Paul Rubens, Flemish;
landscape by Jan Wildens, Flemish, 1586–1653
Jason and the Golden Fleece, c. 1650
Oil on canvas, 6 ft. 4 in. × 10 ft. 7⅜ in.
(1.945 × 3.235 m)
Gift of Julia and Richard H. Rush,
Class of 1937
P.958.251

sachusetts. It differs from the Smith work, however, in its tour-de-force treatment of the figure in motion, a quality that has prompted some scholars to attribute it to another pupil of Lanfranco, Giovanni Battista Beinaschi (1636–1688). P.F.

72 Between 1636 and 1638 the Rubens workshop produced a cycle of paintings based on tales from Ovid's *Metamorphoses* for the hunting lodge of Philip IV of Spain, the Torre de la Parada. Following completion of the commission, themes from the cycle became popular with patrons of Rubens's workshop and among his followers. This *Jason and the Golden Fleece*, illustrating *Metamorphoses* 149–158, is strikingly similar to *Apollo and the Python* of the Torre de la Parada series, painted by Cornelis de Vos from a sketch by Rubens. The Dartmouth painting is a reversal of that composition, with an armored Jason in place of the nude

Apollo. Unlike the Torre de la Parada *Jason*, which depicts the mythological hero removing the fleece from the temple of Mars, the Dartmouth version follows the original Ovid text more closely: it represents Jason's capture of the fleece in the grove of Ares after his conquest of the dragon with a potion of oil. Conservation analysis reveals that the figure's parted hair—a style not common in the seventeenth century—is a later revision. It was perhaps painted over by an owner in the nineteenth century to bring the work in line with current fashion. P.F.

73
George Romney, English, 1734–1802
Portrait of William Henry Irby,
1776–77
Oil on canvas, 29½ × 25 in.
(75.0 × 63.5 cm)
Gift of Julia and Richard H. Rush,
Class of 1937
P.980.72

74
Sir William Beechey, English, 1753–1839
Portrait of Robert Lindley, c. 1810
Oil on canvas, 81 × 57¼ in. (205.7 × 145.4 cm)
Gift of Irving S. Manheimer
P.959.35

73 Among English portraitists of the late eighteenth century, George Romney's stature falls just below that of Thomas Gainsborough and Sir Joshua Reynolds. According to his diaries, Romney began work on this portrait of William Irby (1750–1830), the second son of Baron Boston, in April 1776, with additional sittings in November. By January 1777, the portrait was completed and delivered. Paintings produced between 1775 and 1780, following Romney's trip to Italy, are thought to be among his finest. P.F.

74 A popular portraitist of his day, Sir William Beechey was influenced by the styles of his countrymen Sir Joshua Reynolds and Johannes Zoffany. In 1793 he was honored with the title of portrait painter to Queen Charlotte. The Dartmouth work represents Robert Lindley (1776–1855), a composer, principal cellist for the London Opera from 1794 to 1851, and professor of cello at the Royal Academy of Music, a position he assumed in 1822. Although the painting is undated, given the apparent age of the sitter and similarities between this painting and Beechey's seated portrait of Sir Thomas Livingston Mitchell of about 1808 (Chrysler Museum, Norfolk, Virginia), this portrait probably was executed about 1810. P.F.

75 and 76
Julia Margaret Cameron, English, born India, 1815–1879
Madonna and Child (From Life, Portrait of Mary Hillier) and **From Life, Fresh Water Bay,
Isle of Wight** (from *Portfolio of Twelve Victorian Photographs*), 1865–66
Albumen silver prints from glass negatives,
each 15 × 12 in. (38.1 × 30.5 cm)
75. Inscribed and dated lower left: *From life June 1866*; signed lower right:
Julia Margaret Cameron, Ph.967.96.7
76. Inscribed and dated lower left: *From Life Fresh Water Bay Isle of Wight June 1866*;
signed lower right: *Julia Margaret Cameron*, Ph.967.96.9
Transfer from Sherman Art Library, Dartmouth College

75 and **76** Julia Margaret Cameron began a career late in life photographing her illustrious friends, among them Alfred Tennyson, Thomas Carlyle, and Robert Browning. As an early photographer who approached the art of portraiture much as a painter might, Cameron displayed in her work an intense interest in the personalities of her sitters. Her technique included the use of lenses that are believed to have been specially designed to create soft-focus im-ages. These examples demonstrate Cameron's sentimental religious and allegorical themes and her impressive portrait style. Mary Hillier, who portrayed the Madonna, was Cameron's most frequent model.   J.H.

77
Eugène-Louis-Gabriel Isabey, French, 1803–1886
Seascape, Normandy, 1853(?)
Oil on canvas, 18 × 25¾ in. (45.7 × 65.3 cm)
Signed and dated lower left: *E. Isabey 53*[?]
Gift of Mr. and Mrs. John Pelenyi
P.973.252

78
Sir Lawrence Alma-Tadema, English, born Netherlands, 1836–1912
The Sculpture Garden, 1874
Oil on canvas, 86½ × 67½ in. (219.7 × 171.5 cm)
Signed and inscribed lower right: *Alma-Tadema op. cxxv*
Gift of Arthur M. Loew, Class of 1921A
P.961.125

77 A Romantic landscape painter and contemporary of Eugène Delacroix, Eugène Isabey was noted for his seascapes of the French coast. Trips to England with Delacroix and Richard Parkes Bonington in 1825, and to Holland and Belgium in 1839 and again in 1846, acquainted the artist with the British and northern European traditions of landscape painting. Combining those styles with his own experience of the French seaside, Isabey developed a type of marine painting that influenced Johan Barthold Jongkind and Eugène Boudin, artists with whom he worked in the 1840s. This seascape, which depicts the departure of fishermen in Normandy, probably dates from the mid-1850s. Isabey had purchased property in Normandy, and the site became a popular theme in his art during that period. As a predecessor of the Impressionists, Isabey helped to popularize sites at Dieppe, Honfleur, Le Havre, and Trouville in landscape painting of the 1850s and 1860s.   P.F.

78 Cited by Lawrence Alma-Tadema's contemporary biographer, Edmund Gosse, as one of the artist's most famous works, this painting was executed in Rome in 1874. *The Sculpture Garden*, which is set in ancient Rome, can be read as a historicized metaphor for the artist's own profession. It represents a servant, identified by the crescent-shaped ornament at his neck, turning a sculpture toward aristocratic patrons for approval. Alma-Tadema himself identified these figures as "portraits of myself and my family." The seated gentleman represents the painter, the woman and children, his wife Laura, who was also a painter, and his two daughters. The woman at left may portray his first wife, Marie Gressin. Autobiographical depictions of the artist's working environment were common in Alma-Tadema's paintings of 1867 to 1877.

Born in Friesland and trained in Belgium, Alma-Tadema carried his academic style to tremendous success in England, where he settled and obtained citizenship in the 1870s. When *The Sculpture Garden* was exhibited at the Royal Academy in 1875, however, the critic John Ruskin responded with mixed praise, describing it as "a work showing artistic skill and classical learning, both in a high degree. . . . The artistic skill has succeeded with all its objects in the degree of their unimportance. . . . The execution is dextrous but more with mechanical steadiness of practice than innate fineness of nerve."   P.F.

79
Constantin Guys, French, 1802–1892
Girl for Hire (Demoiselle à Vendre)
Black chalk, pen and brown ink, colored washes,
8½ × 6⅝ in. (21.6 × 16.7 cm)
Gift of Abby Aldrich Rockefeller
W.935.1.23

80
Pierre-Auguste Renoir, French, 1841–1919
Standing Nude Figure, c. 1890
Red, white, and black Conté crayon on buff paper,
13¾ × 3¾ in. (34.9 × 9.4 cm)
Signed upper right: *Renoir.*
Bequest of Harold G. Rugg, Class of 1906
D.957.116

79 When Charles Baudelaire wrote his famous essay "The Painter of Modern Life" in 1863, he held up Constantin Guys as the model of his ideal. As an artist who worked almost exclusively in watercolor and an illustrator of popular journals and newspapers, Guys exemplified for Baudelaire the naïve observer and transcriber of modern society. This watercolor reveals the qualities that the writer most admired: a contemporary subject (the courtesan luring a client), a freshness of execution (fluid pen and ink wash), and an individualized response to the subject, which in a few gestural strokes conveys more than a photographic description could.   P.F.

80 This drawing by the nineteenth-century artist Pierre-Auguste Renoir in the eighteenth-century "trois crayons" manner reflects the academic bent of the artist's career. Having begun his association with Claude Monet, Camille Pissarro, and Edgar Degas in the 1860s, Renoir joined in the formation of the Impressionists' first exhibition in 1874. By the late 1870s, however, Renoir had begun to retreat from the avant-garde style and subject matter of his colleagues and sought to establish his art in a more conservative vein. A trip to Italy in 1881 and academic studies of the nude followed. This undated drawing relates to a series of studies for *The Bathers* of 1887 (Philadelphia Museum of Art) and also to similar studies of the nude executed in the mid-1890s.   P.F.

81

Camille Pissarro,
French, 1830–1903
**Girls at a Flower
Fair, Dieppe,** 1901
Gouache on fabric
on paper,
9½ × 8 in.
(24.1 × 20.2 cm)
Signed and dated
lower left:
C Pissarro 1901;
inscribed lower
right: *Dieppe*
Gift of Josephine
and Ivan Albright,
Class of 1978H
P.980.62

81 The subject of the rural market scene is a recurrent one in Camille Pissarro's oeuvre; examples include *The Poultry Market, Gisors*, 1885 (Museum of Fine Arts, Boston), and the *Market at Gisors* series from 1894–95. The setting of the Dartmouth work is the bustling, urbanized port of Dieppe. In a letter of 1901 the artist wrote that he was searching for new motifs, a quest that had taken him to Dieppe. The style of this gouache is characteristic of Pissarro's late phase in its loose handling of the brush, high-keyed palette, and abbreviated treatment of the faces. This work reflects the return Pissarro made near the end of his life to the Impressionist style of the 1870s.   P.F.

82
Edouard Vuillard, French, 1868—1940
Seascape at Honfleur (Marine à Honfleur), 1904
Oil on paper board, mounted on Masonite,
23 × 15½ in. (58.4 × 39.4 cm)
Signed lower right: *E. Vuillard*
Gift of Evelyn A. and William B. Jaffe,
Class of 1964H
P.954.92

Henri de Toulouse-Lautrec, French, 1864—1901
The Jockey, 1899
Lithograph printed in six colors,
20⅜ × 14¼ in. (51.6 × 36.2 cm)
Signed and dated in reverse in the stone,
lower right: *HTL* [monogram] *1899*;
inscribed in pencil, lower right: *205 lm*
Gift of Daisy Shapiro in memory of her son,
Richard David Shapiro, Class of 1943
Pr.966.44

83
Paul Cézanne, French, 1839—1906
Woman at Her Toilette, c. 1883—86
Pencil and watercolor on paper,
6¼ × 5¼ in. (15.8 × 13.3 cm)
Gift of Josephine and Ivan Albright, Class of 1978H,
in honor of Churchill P. Lathrop
W.978.175

82 An artist who matured with the Nabi movement of the late 1880s, Vuillard in his early works used a technique of short daubs of color that describe decorative, patterned interiors. Around 1900, however, Vuillard's style changed. Patterned brushstrokes gave way to broader planes of color; his subjects were expanded from intimate interiors to include marines and rural and urban landscapes. As exemplified by this seascape, in his later work Vuillard sought to recapture the subjects and style of an earlier generation of Impressionists.   P.F.

83 Among the Impressionists only Paul Cézanne and Pierre-Auguste Renoir shared an interest in monumental compositions of the nude. Unlike the majority of his Impressionist colleagues, however, Cézanne often worked through his ideas extensively in drawing and watercolor. Beginning with small studies of single nude figures in the mid-1870s, Cézanne's interest in the subject culminated in large compositional groupings of bathers produced during the last decade of his life. This long period of experimentation has posed problems for scholars who have attempted to place these studies in the artist's oeuvre. The pose of the figure in

Woman at Her Toilette—a nude with upraised arms—is recurrent in the artist's drawings and watercolors, further confounding the question of date. This sketch thus has been variously dated: 1879—82 by Lionello Venturi, 1872—74 in a subsequent revision of Venturi's text, and about 1895 by John Rewald in his recent catalogue of the artist's watercolors. The technique—repeated pencil lines outlining the figure, the scrawled

gestural fall of the figure's hair, as well as a relatively high degree of detail in the sketch—would seem to find its closest parallel in two drawings that have been dated by Adrien Chappuis to 1878–81 and 1883–86, and we have tentatively assigned the sketch to that second span of years. On the reverse of this watercolor is an extremely abbreviated landscape sketch.   P.F.

84 Henri de Toulouse-Lautrec began his career as a painter in Paris during the early 1880s. A thoroughly cosmopolitan artist with links to the commercial world of the dance halls and other forms of popular entertainment, Toulouse-Lautrec turned in the early 1890s to lithography in the form of posters, song sheets, and single-sheet prints for collectors. In lithography he found a sympathetic medium for his expressive line, strong sense of decoration, and trenchant social

insight. This print was to have been one of a series of racetrack subjects. Although Toulouse-Lautrec drew other compositions for the series, his health did not allow him to continue it; he died less than two years later. *The Jockey* was published in two editions, one in black and white and one in color. J.B.

AMERICAN ART

THE art collection of Dartmouth College began with American works, and today the Hood Museum can claim an extensive inventory of American painting, sculpture, and decorative arts. The college's strength in this area stems from its two-hundred-year tradition of commemorating events and people with objects or portraits made in New England. In recent decades the American holdings at Dartmouth have developed further through the efforts of art faculty, alumni, and museum staff.

The first art object donated to Dartmouth College was the silver monteith (number 88) presented by the royal governor of New Hampshire, John Wentworth, to the college's founder and first president, Eleazar Wheelock, in honor of the first commencement in 1771. This handsome bowl, fashioned by Boston silversmith Daniel Henchman, eventually became a focal point of an extensive collection of American arts at Dartmouth. Like the scores of portraits of college officials and associates that the school acquired during the following century and a half, the monteith has been valued not only for its aesthetic merits, but also for its historical significance to the institution.

Joseph Steward's life-size portraits of Eleazar Wheelock and college trustee John Phillips (numbers 85 and 86), both completed in 1796, were the first of many likenesses of Dartmouth leaders to be commissioned by the college. About forty years later a group of four noteworthy portraits immortalized the college's legal counsel—Daniel Webster, Jeremiah Mason, Jeremiah Smith, and Joseph Hopkinson—who had successfully defended the original charter of the institution against those who wished to restructure it as a state university. *The Trustees of Dartmouth College* v. *William H. Woodward* was argued in the New Hampshire courts in 1817 and was finally resolved in favor of the college by the United States Supreme Court in 1819. In terms of its ramifications both for contract law and the future of the college, the court's decision was pivotal. Within a matter of months the trustees arranged for portraits of the four counselors who, in a sense, had refounded the institution. The trustees' first choice as artist was the well-established Gilbert Stuart. For reasons unknown, Stuart did not carry out the commission before his death in 1828, and the project languished until the mid-1830s. At that time an enthusiastic alumnus, George Cheyne Shattuck, offered to make the necessary arrangements to commission and donate the portraits to the college. The four oil paintings, finally completed in 1835, consist of Thomas Sully's graceful depiction of Joseph Hopkinson, Chester Harding's forthright portrait of Jeremiah Mason, Francis Alexander's likeness of Jeremiah Smith, and the same artist's romantic portrayal of Daniel Webster (number 96), the college's most famous and eloquent defender.

Other college-related portrait commissions and donations followed over the next century, and by the 1930s Dartmouth could boast a surprisingly extensive survey of works by some of the nation's leading portraitists, including Gilbert Stuart, John Vanderlyn, John Wesley Jarvis, Samuel F. B. Morse, George Peter A. Healy, and Joseph DeCamp.

One of the first and most notable gifts of American painting outside the realm of portraiture was Frederic Remington's *Shotgun Hospitality* (number 105), presented in 1909, just one year after the canvas was completed. The topical interest of the painting initially overshadowed its artistic value. The donor, Judge Horace Russell, class of 1865, apparently thought its Native American subject matter would hold particular appeal for the college in light of Eleazar Wheelock's original mission to educate Indians. Eight years later Dartmouth received its first landscapes by American artists: large-scale Arcadian views of the Italian countryside by William Sonntag (number 99) and George Loring Brown, both donated by an Annie B. Dore.

It was not until early in the twentieth century that a growing faculty began to take an aggressive role in developing the fine arts collection and in sponsoring temporary art exhibitions for the benefit of students. In 1916, largely under the leadership of art professor George Breed Zug, the college organized the first group exhibition of artists working in nearby Cornish, New Hampshire. Daniel Chester French's bust of Ralph Waldo Emerson, included in the exhibition, was presented to the college by the sculptor a few years later. During the 1920s Professor Zug and others encouraged additional gifts and initiated purchases as well, particularly in the area of prints. A notable addition in those years was the gift in 1929 of ten John Singer Sargent drawings, studies for a mural in the Boston Public Library, from the artist's sisters, Emily Sargent and Violet Ormond.

The greatest catalyst for the development of the American collection at Dartmouth—and its art holdings in general—was Abby Aldrich Rockefeller's gift in 1935 of over one hundred examples of contemporary art, American folk art, and Native American watercolors. This gift included the college's only work by Thomas Eakins (number 110), the endearing carved baseball figure attributed to Thomas Brooks (number 104), and many fine works of nineteenth-century naïve painting and sculpture.

Other gifts to the collection soon followed as a direct consequence of Mrs. Rockefeller's donation. In 1938 and again in 1940, art collector and patron Preston Harrison gave the college several modern works, as well as an earlier watercolor by Maurice Prendergast (number 108) and a small oil by William Merritt Chase (number 106). In 1939 Harrison wrote to Churchill Lathrop, then chairman of the department of art and archaeology, "Mrs. Rockefeller had the right idea—[she] gave the key cue— so I took it up with Dartmouth."

During the past five decades, as funds designated specifically for the purchase of art gradually have become available, the college has directed the growth of its American collection in a more deliberate manner. For example, the Julia L. Whittier Fund, established in 1940, has allowed the college to acquire numerous works of art representing diverse mediums, periods, and nationalities. Among the most significant American art works purchased through this fund during the 1950s and 1960s were several paintings depicting New Hampshire's White Mountains. These landscapes, by such artists as George Loring Brown, W. W. Brown, Benjamin Champney, Thomas Doughty (number 98), William Hart, John Henry Hill, and Frank Henry Shapleigh, comprise an unusually extensive study collection. The recent gift of Régis Gignoux's monumental *New Hampshire* (number 102) is a notable addition.

Among the major gifts of American art to come to the college since the 1960s are the exquisite pastel of Governor John Wentworth by John Singleton Copley (number 87), an oil portrait by Rembrandt Peale, landscapes by Alexander H. Wyant, William Mason Brown, George Inness, and Ernest Lawson, as well as numerous prints and drawings. Recent donations of sculpture include a bronze figure of Daniel Webster by Thomas Ball (an artist already represented in the collection by several portrait busts) and two bronzes by Frederic Remington.

In a manner paralleling the early growth of the American painting collection, American decorative arts originally were acquired by the college either as accessories for campus buildings or as memorabilia of former college associates. Two especially noteworthy gifts of furniture were the bequest in 1928 of Edwin Webster Sanborn, class of 1878, which featured several fine examples of New Hampshire and coastal New England cabinetmaking; and a 1946 donation by Mrs. William Dexter of Neoclassical furnishings from the library of the Boston home of George Ticknor, class of 1807 (see number 97). In recent years, and partly as a result of the 1981 exhibition and catalogue *American Decorative Arts at Dartmouth* (organized by the museum's registrar at the time, Margaret J. Moody), several pieces have been rediscovered not only as important historical artifacts, but also as instructive and worthy examples of New England craftsmanship.

Dartmouth's greatest source of pride in the area of American decorative arts is the extraordinary collection of early New England silver donated over the last three decades by Louise C. and Frank L. Harrington, class of 1924. Nearly all of the pieces in the Harrington Collection were made in Massachusetts, primarily Boston, during the eighteenth century; included are notable examples by some of the commonwealth's most talented silversmiths: Jeremiah Dummer (number 89), John Coney, John Burt (number 91), Benjamin Burt, Jacob Hurd, and Paul Revere II (number 90).

Today Dartmouth's American paintings and decorative arts constitute one of its strongest collections. Through judicious development of these holdings and the sponsorship of related exhibitions, the Hood Museum continues to affirm its commitment to American art, a commitment that is nearly as old as the college itself.   B.J.M.

85
Joseph Steward, American, 1753–1822
Portrait of Eleazar Wheelock, 1793–96
Oil on canvas, 79⅛ × 69⅞ in. (201.0 × 177.5 cm)
Signed lower left on baseboard: *J. Steward Pinxt.*
Commissioned by the Trustees of Dartmouth College
P.793.2

86
Joseph Steward, American, 1753–1822
Portrait of John Phillips, 1794–96
Oil on canvas, 79¼ × 68½ in. (201.3 × 174.0 cm)
Signed lower left on base of pilaster: *J. Steward. Pinxt.*
Commissioned by the Trustees of Dartmouth College
P.793.1

87
John Singleton Copley, American, 1738–1815
Portrait of Governor John Wentworth, 1769
Pastel on paper mounted on canvas, 23 × 17½ in. (58.5 × 44.4 cm)
Signed and dated center right: *JSC* [monogram] *p. 1769.*
Gift of Esther Lowell Abbott in memory of her husband, Gordon Abbott
D.977.175

85 This portrait of Eleazar Wheelock (1711–1779), founder and first president of Dartmouth College, was commissioned by the college trustees about thirteen years after the sitter's death. This painting and the portrait of John Phillips (number 86), also by Steward, were the first in a long series of commissioned works depicting Dartmouth presidents, trustees, faculty, and students.

A graduate of the college himself, Steward may have painted his former instructor from memory, or he may have referred to an earlier miniature of the sitter, now lost.

Steward turned to painting in 1788 following a brief career in the ministry. Although he had some art instruction from John Trumbull, Steward's primary influence seems to have been the painter Ralph Earl, a portraitist who, like Steward, worked in the Connecticut River Valley.   B.J.M.

86 John Phillips was a trustee of Dartmouth College for twenty years and founder of Phillips Exeter Academy in Exeter, New Hampshire. This portrait was commissioned by the college in 1793 on the occasion of Phillips's retirement as trustee. Unlike the posthumous portrait of Eleazar Wheelock (number 85), which Steward may have painted from memory, this likeness was drawn by Steward from life in the sitter's hometown of Exeter. According to minutes from the annual meeting of the college trustees in 1793, Steward agreed to paint the portrait "at the price of twelve guineas including his expenses of travelling to & from Exeter for the purpose." In a letter dated November 5, 1793, Steward postponed starting the portrait until the following February.   B.J.M.

87 This forthright, sensitive pastel portrait of New Hampshire's last royal governor, John Wentworth (1737–1820), was drawn when both sitter and artist, John Singleton Copley, were thirty-two years of age and at the heights of their careers. In 1766 Copley expressed a preference for pastels in a letter to Benjamin West ("I think my best portraits [have been] done in that way"); yet of the hundreds of likenesses he completed during his lifetime, only forty in this delicate me-dium are known. Nearly all of his pastels, including this portrayal of Wentworth, were done between 1765 and 1770. Despite Copley's lack of formal training, his extraordi-nary artistic talent brought him prestige and prosperity both in America and in England, where he spent the last forty years of his life.

The sitter, Royal Governor Wentworth, was popular with New Hampshire colonists for sympathizing with their opposition to the heavy taxes imposed by the British Parlia-ment. He granted Eleazar Wheelock the charter for Dartmouth College in 1769 and later gave to him "and to his Successors" in office a silver monteith (number 88) in honor of the college's first commencement in 1771. Wentworth eventually took a stand against the colonists' resistance to the British and fled to England at the outbreak of the American Revolution. In 1783 he returned to North America as lieutenant governor of Nova Scotia.   B.J.M.

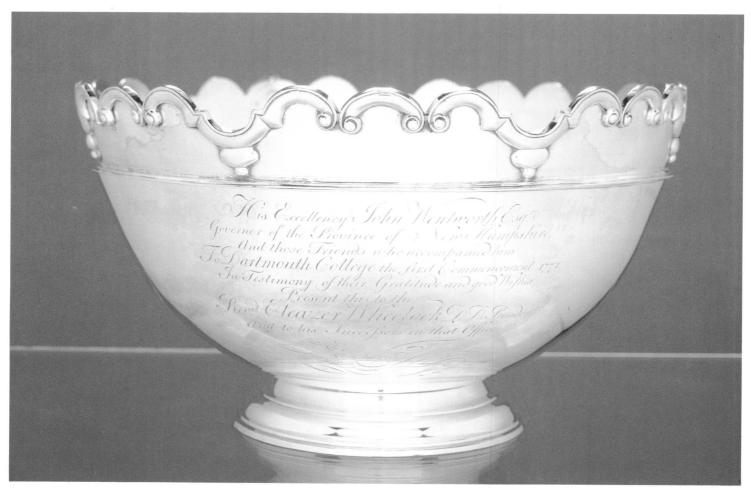

88

Daniel Henchman, American, 1730–1775
Engraved by Nathaniel Hurd, American, 1729/30–1777
Monteith, 1771–73
Silver, h. 6⅛ in. (15.5 cm), diam. 10¾ in. (27.5 cm)
Marked on bottom: *Henchman* [in rectangle]; engraved in calligraphic design on bowl's side: *N.H. scp*
Engraved: *His Excellency John Wentworth Esq*ʳ., / *Governor of the Province of New Hampshire,* /
And those Friends who accompanied him / *To Dartmouth College the first Commencement 1771.* /
In Testimony of their Gratitude and good Wishes / *Present this to the* /
*Rev*ᵈ. *Eleazer Wheelock, D.D. President* / *And to his Successors in that Office.*
Gift of John Wentworth, Royal Governor of New Hampshire
M.773.1

88 As the grantor of Dartmouth College's charter, Royal Governor John Wentworth followed the school's development with special interest. He recognized that its first commencement ceremony of 1771, modest though it was, marked a significant achievement on the part of the institution's founder, Eleazar Wheelock. To commemorate the event Wentworth chose to honor Wheelock and his presidential successors with a monteith fashioned by Boston silversmith Daniel Henchman and engraved by Henchman's brother-in-law, Nathaniel Hurd. It was completed and presented to President Wheelock in 1773.

A monteith is a large bowl with a notched rim that was used in the eighteenth century to chill wine glasses or rinse them between courses. Although the form was popular in England during the late seventeenth and early eighteenth centuries, only two other Colonial American monteiths are known, both of them made by Boston silversmith John Coney. Dartmouth's monteith has come to be regarded as the undisputed masterpiece of Daniel Henchman's career and one of the finest examples of Colonial American silver.   B.J.M.

89 Jeremiah Dummer of Boston is the earliest American-born silversmith (or goldsmith, as he would have described himself) whose work has survived. He served as an apprentice to the first goldsmiths known to have worked in this country, John Hull and Robert Sanderson, who emigrated from England in the 1630s and established a partnership in Boston in 1652. This tankard by Dummer, with its architectural proportions and exuberant cast ornament, is characteristic of seventeenth-century silver made in the Colonies and England. The inspiration for this fanciful form of decoration was the then-popular

89
Jeremiah Dummer, American, 1645–1718
Tankard, c. 1690
Silver, h. including thumbpiece 7⅝ in. (19.4 cm),
diam. of base 5⅝ in. (14.2 cm)
Marked on cover, on body at left of handle, and on bottom:
ID [with fleur-de-lis below, in a heart-shaped punch];
engraved on handle: *RR*; on bottom in script: *Mrs. / Rebecca Russell*
Gift of Louise C. and Frank L. Harrington, Class of 1924
M.970.77

90
Paul Revere II, American, 1735–1818
Water Pitcher, 1804
Silver, h. 6¼ in. (15.8 cm), diam. of base 4 in. (10.0 cm)
Marked on bottom: *REVERE* [in clipped-corner rectangle];
engraved beneath spout: *BRAY / 1804*
Gift of Louise C. and Frank L. Harrington, Class of 1924
M.966.116

91
John Burt, American, 1692–1745/46
Salver, c. 1725
Silver, h. 1¾ in. (4.5 cm), diam. of dish, 5¾ in. (14.7 cm)
Marked on top near rim: *I:BURT* [in cartouche]
Gift of Louise C. and Frank L. Harrington, Class of 1924
M.971.22

Anglo-Netherlandish adaptation of sixteenth-century Mannerism. Like Hull and Sanderson, as well as other New England goldsmiths of this period, Dummer was capable of fashioning silver equal in sophistication to the finest English plate.   B.J.M.

90 Immortalized in Henry Wadsworth Longfellow's poem "The Midnight Ride of Paul Revere," Boston patriot Paul Revere is America's most famous silversmith. The son of French-born Apollos Rivoire, from whom he learned his trade, Revere achieved renown

for his skillful engraving as well as his silversmithing. This jug was made for Major John Bray (c. 1761–1829) of Boston, as were two beakers by Benjamin Burt in the college collection, similarly engraved but dated 1797. The shape of this elegantly proportioned pitcher undoubtedly was inspired by transfer-printed creamware jugs imported from England and popular in America after 1800. Twelve of Revere's pitchers of this type are known today, but the form has been copied by others nearly as often as his well-known Sons of Liberty bowl of 1768.   B.J.M.

91 This diminutive hexafoil salver with a trumpet base, used to serve wafers, biscuits, mints, or drinks, is believed to be the only one of its kind among documented American silver. Its maker, John Burt, was a native of Boston who most likely served his apprenticeship with the prominent Boston goldsmith John Coney. Burt trained three of his sons, Samuel, William, and Benjamin, to follow his profession.   B.J.M.

92
American, Eastern Massachusetts
Dressing Table, 1730–50
Walnut veneer and maple with pine,
31 × 35 × 20⅜ in. (78.7 × 88.7 × 51.7 cm)
Gift of Louise C. and Frank L. Harrington,
Class of 1924
F.974.360

93
Attributed to Julius Barnard, American, 1769–18??
Sideboard, 1801
Mahogany and satinwood veneers on white pine and spruce,
40 × 74 × 27½ in. (101.6 × 187.9 × 69.8 cm)
Bequest of Philip H. Chase
F.980.64

---

92 Dressing tables came into fashion in England during the William and Mary period of the late seventeenth and early eighteenth centuries, often as companion pieces to high chests of drawers. This handsome Massachusetts example combines the rectilinear characteristics of the William and Mary style with the graceful outlines of the subsequent Queen Anne style. The attention to surface decoration, demonstrated by the figured veneers and herringbone inlays, is typical of William and Mary style furniture made in this country during the first quarter of the eighteenth century. Traits of the later, Queen Anne fashion, however—which began to exert its influence on American furnishings around 1730—can be seen in the cabriole legs, pad feet, and shaped skirt of this table.   B.J.M.

93 This sideboard belonged to Mills Olcott (1774–1845), treasurer of Dartmouth College from 1816 to 1822 and a prominent Hanover lawyer and businessman. Julius Barnard is thought to have been the maker because he briefly operated a cabinetmaking shop in Hanover in 1801; this was also a year in which, according to the Olcott papers in Dartmouth's Baker Library, Barnard frequently exchanged goods and services with Olcott. In 1802 Barnard moved his trade to Windsor, Vermont, where in 1805 he advertised the production of "sash-cornered, commode & strait-front sideboards." The innovative arrangement of inlays on this piece places it in the tradition of rural cabinetmaking of the Connecticut River Valley; yet its elegant outlines and sophisticated craftsmanship demonstrate that Barnard was attuned to the high-style furniture fashions emanating from urban centers.   B.J.M.

94

Benjamin West,
American, 1738–1820

**Archangel Gabriel of the
Annunciation**, 1784

Pen and ink with red and
blue chalk, 17⅜ × 12⅛ in.
(44.1 × 30.8 cm)

Signed and dated lower right:
B. West. 1784.

Julia L. Whittier Fund

D.959.104

94 Benjamin West was the first native American artist to study art abroad and achieve international standing in his profession. Although he spent most of his career in England, he wielded tremendous influence on American art through his promotion of history painting and through his many American protégés, among them Gilbert Stuart, Washington Allston, John Trumbull, and Samuel F. B. Morse. This drawing, executed in a fluid, calligraphic manner, dates from the artist's most prolific and artistically successful period.   B.J.M.

95
Chester Harding, American, 1792–1866
Portrait of Mrs. Daniel Webster, 1827
Oil on canvas, 36 × 29 in. (91.5 × 73.6 cm)
Gift of the William L. Bryant Foundation
P.953.28

97
Thomas Sully, American, 1783–1872
Portrait of George Ticknor, 1831
Oil on canvas, 36 × 28 in. (91.5 × 71.1 cm)
Signed and dated lower left: *TS. 1831.*
Gift of Constance V. R. White, Nathaniel T. Dexter,
Philip Dexter, and Mary Ann Streeter
P.943.130

96
Francis Alexander, American, 1800–1880
Portrait of Daniel Webster ("Black Dan"), 1835
Oil on canvas, 30 × 25 in. (76.2 × 63.5 cm)
Signed, inscribed, and dated on reverse:
Painted by Fr. Alexander for Dartmouth at Boston, 1835
Gift of George C. Shattuck, Class of 1803
P.836.3

95 Considering his humble beginnings as a sign painter and his initial lack of formal training, Chester Harding achieved remarkable success as a portraitist in his lifetime. His extraordinary popularity—described during his day as "Harding fever"—brought him over one thousand portrait commissions. Harding's renderings of female sitters are perhaps his most sympathetic, as demonstrated in this becoming portrait of Daniel

Webster's first wife, Grace Fletcher (1781–1828). In December of 1827, a few months after Harding's return to America from a three-year stay in England, he wrote to his friend S. F. Lyman about this recently completed picture: "Although I have been so much taken . . . in playing the man of business, I have done several portraits, one in particular of Mrs. Daniel Webster, which has elicited from her husband a voluntary promise that he will sit to me the moment he returns from this political campaign." Dartmouth also owns the companion portrait of Webster, done in 1832. Mrs. Webster, who

died only a year after this portrait was completed, is shown fashionably dressed in an outfit made for the cornerstone-laying ceremonies of the Bunker Hill Monument in Charlestown, Massachusetts, in 1825. Webster's oration on that occasion has been considered the most eloquent summary of the principles behind the American Revolution.   B.J.M.

96 Daniel Webster (1782–1825), class of 1801, was adopted as Dartmouth's "second founder" when in 1818 he eloquently and successfully defended the college's original charter in the United States Supreme Court, arguing against those who wished to have the private institution restructured as a state university. With the assistance of alumnus Dr. George Shattuck, Dartmouth honored Webster and the three other members of the college case counsel with handsome portraits painted by Francis Alexander, Thomas Sully, and Chester Harding (see also pages 13 and 102).

In what is by far the most theatrical and penetrating of the countless surviving portraits of Webster, Alexander sets the swarthy orator, known as "Black Dan," against an energized, fiery sky. By use of a low vantage point he accentuates Webster's immense forehead, tousled hair, and fervent gaze, suggesting the statesman's electrifying presence and his celebrated powers of reason. B.J.M.

97 In his mastery of flamboyant brushwork, dramatic poses, and idealization of form, Sully reveals his admiration for his early mentor, Gilbert Stuart, and the debt owed to his English instructor, the Romantic portraitist Thomas Lawrence. Sully's likeness of George Ticknor (1791–1871), class of 1807, a distinguished man of letters and a founder of the Boston Public Library, displays the mix of refinement and vigor that characterizes the artist's most memorable portraits.   B.J.M.

98
Thomas Doughty, American, 1793–1856
Rowing on a Mountain Lake, c. 1835
Oil on canvas, 17 × 14 in. (43.2 × 35.7 cm)
Signed lower left: *T. Doughty*
Julia L. Whittier Fund
P.967.88

99
William Louis Sonntag, American, 1822–1899
Italian Lake with Classical Ruins, 1858
Oil on canvas on aluminum panel,
35¾ × 60 in. (90.8 × 152.3 cm)
Dated lower left: *'58*
Gift of Annie B. Dore
P.917.3

100
Elihu Vedder, American, 1836–1923
The Fisherman and the Mermaid, 1879
Oil on canvas, 16½ × 28½ in. (42.0 × 72.5 cm)
Signed and dated lower left: *E. Vedder—1879*
Gift of Dana and Miroslav J. Polak
P.982.53

98 A precursor, if not an early member, of the Hudson River School, Thomas Doughty is remembered for his idealized sylvan landscapes that depict man at peace with his natural surroundings. Yet Doughty was equally capable of describing more provocative moments, as exemplified by this radiant early-morning scene in the White Mountains. In the Romantic tradition, the blasted tree and threatening clouds add a note of tension to this otherwise placid composition, reinforcing the theme of man's insignificance in the face of nature.   B.J.M.

99 Rich in historical and artistic associations, Italy held great romantic appeal for aspiring nineteenth-century American artists. Like many of his contemporaries, William Sonntag made frequent and extended pilgrimages there, attracted more by the romanticized ideal of the nation's past than by the realities of its complex and unglamorous present. This poetic scene, which includes a ruin based on the temple of Vesta in Tivoli, was probably painted from sketches Sonntag made during his year-long stay in 1855–56. At least two other versions of the same scene are known, including a slightly larger

composition in the collection of the Corcoran Gallery of Art, Washington, D.C. B.J.M.

100 Elihu Vedder's melancholic and highly personal interpretation of a traditional mythological theme distinguishes this composition from the strictly historical subjects of many of his late-nineteenth-century contemporaries. His visionary effects were achieved largely through the use of dramatic lighting, metallic colors, and bold, sinuous lines reminiscent of the work of English Pre-Raphaelite painters such as Dante Gabriel Rossetti. B.J.M.

101
Norton Bush, American, 1834–1894
Lake Nicaragua, 1871
Oil on canvas, 20¼ × 36 in. (51.4 × 91.5 cm)
Signed and dated lower left: *NB* [monogram] *USH. 1871.*
Julia L. Whittier Fund
P.970.56

102
Régis Francois Gignoux, French, 1814–1882
New Hampshire (White Mountain Landscape), c. 1864
Oil on canvas, 48 × 83¾ in. (121.8 × 212.8 cm)
Purchase made possible by a gift of Olivia H. and John O.
Parker, Class of 1958, and by the Julia L. Whittier Fund
P.961.1

101 One of the lesser-known American Luminists, Norton Bush was a California artist who specialized in tropical landscapes. The minutely detailed foliage of *Lake Nicaragua* reveals Bush's early training with the Hudson River School painter Jasper Cropsey. The painting's serene, orderly composition and crystalline light, however, owe more to Bush's contemporary Martin Johnson Heade and to the more renowned painter of tropical scenes Frederic Edwin Church. As with Church's tropical subjects, *Lake Nicaragua* reflects North America's political,

scientific, and artistic interest in the South American continent in the mid- and late nineteenth century.   B.J.M.

102 Despite his remarkable success as a painter of the American landscape and his close association with leading artists of his day, the French-born Régis François Gignoux is generally cited in art-history surveys solely for his role as the teacher of George Inness—a position he occupied for only one month. Trained at Lyons and later Paris, Gignoux is said to have left France in pursuit of his future wife, Elizabeth Christmas, who

in 1840 returned to America from a visit abroad. Like the Hudson River School painters already established here, Gignoux traveled deep into the wilderness of the Adirondacks and the White Mountains in search of subjects for his paintings. At the same time he received numerous commissions for his charming skating scenes, which, like their seventeenth-century Netherlandish counterparts, were usually set in nonspecific, idealized locales.

Although suggestions have been made as to the location depicted in *New Hampshire*, this majestic landscape more likely is a

103
George Inness, American, 1825–1894
In the Gloaming, 1893
Oil on canvas, 22 × 27⅛ in. (55.9 × 68.9 cm)
Signed and dated lower right: *G. Inness 1893*
Gift of Clement S. Houghton
P.948.44

romanticized composite view inspired by Gignoux's visits to the Presidential Range in New Hampshire's White Mountains, liberally embellished for dramatic effect. Its sweeping vista, deep recession into space, and mastery of atmospheric effects reveal Gignoux's admiration for his more influential contemporaries Frederic Edwin Church and Albert Bierstadt, both of whom he knew as fellow tenants at the Tenth Street Studio Building in New York City. Like Church, Gignoux was highly regarded for his views of Niagara Falls.

He painted versions of the popular site as early as 1847—ten years before Church completed his enormously successful *Niagara Falls*. Two of Gignoux's Niagara paintings were exhibited alongside Church's acclaimed canvas, one in 1859 and one in 1860, and were favorably compared to the well-known masterpiece.   B.J.M.

103 *In the Gloaming* dates from George Inness's most fruitful, late years, during which he painted his rural environs near Montclair, New Jersey. Like many of his late works, *In the Gloaming* exhibits a restricted, subdued palette, rich glazing, and an enveloping mist that almost obscures form. Although Inness clearly concerned himself with the effects of light and atmosphere, he scorned the analytic approach of his Impressionist contemporaries. His poetic canvases reflect instead an intensely personal, almost mystical exploration of the larger significance of the landscape.   B.J.M.

104
Attributed to Thomas V. Brooks, American, 1828–1895
Baseball Player (Shop Sign), c. 1870–75
Polychromed wood, h. with base 70½ in. (179.1 cm)
Gift of Abby Aldrich Rockefeller
S.935.1.113

105
Frederic Remington, American, 1861–1909
Shotgun Hospitality, 1908
Oil on canvas, 27 × 40 in. (68.5 × 101.4 cm)
Signed and dated lower right: *Frederic Remington / 1908—*
Gift of Judge Horace Russell, Class of 1865
P.909.2

104 Abby Aldrich Rockefeller gave this base-ball figure to Dartmouth College in 1935, having purchased the work from Edith Gregor Halpert, a New York dealer and pioneer in the collecting of American folk art. Correspondence with Mrs. Halpert indicates that the figure came from Bridgeport, Connecticut, where it had been used as a trade sign for a sporting goods store. The work has been attributed on stylistic grounds to Thomas Brooks, who operated a flourishing carving business in New York from 1847 until moving to Chicago in 1878.   B.J.M.

105 Although Frederic Remington achieved unprecedented success as an illustrator of the American West early in his career, he did not feel he had arrived as a full-fledged painter until his final years. In *Shotgun Hospitality*, completed a year before his death, Remington has transcended pure narrative through his dramatic manipulation of the campfire light and his subtle modulation of nocturnal hues.   B.J.M.

106
William Merritt Chase, American, 1849–1916
The Lone Fisherman, 1890s
Oil on panel, 15 × 11⅞ in. (38.1 × 30.1 cm)
Signed lower left: *WM* [monogram] *M. Chase*
Gift of Mr. and Mrs. Preston Harrison
P.940.40

107
James McNeill Whistler, American, 1834–1903
Maud in Bed, 1884–86
Watercolor, gouache, and pencil on cardboard,
9⅞ × 7 in. (25.1 × 17.6 cm)
Signed with butterfly device upper right
Gift of Mr. and Mrs. Arthur E. Allen, Jr., Class of 1932
W.971.26

---

106 In a letter dated 1939, the donor of this painting, Preston Harrison, wrote to Churchill Lathrop, the director of Dartmouth's art galleries, of his most recent gift to the college: "The other small painting . . . is by William M. Chase—now in 'Dutch' with your out and out modernist. I bought this in 1916 direct from Chase in his New York studio— and paid plenty too. It is on a mahogany panel—a most peculiar subject—Shinnecock Canal (near his [Chase's] home)—a huge riprap of immense stones on one side. Chase's father about 85 at time is sitting on a rock . . . fishing in canal."

Chase operated his summer school of art at Shinnecock, Long Island, from 1891 to 1902. There, and through his instruction at the Art Students League of New York, the Pennsylvania Academy of the Fine Arts, Philadelphia, and his teaching tours of Europe, he inspired hundreds of students. Although many of his pupils imitated his modified Impressionist style, others went on to become leaders of American Modernism—Charles Demuth, Charles Sheeler, and Georgia O'Keeffe among them.   B.J.M.

107 James McNeill Whistler, perhaps the most influential American artist of his gener-

ation, spent most of his career in Europe, dividing his time between Paris and London. Born in Lowell, Massachusetts, Whistler moved to Paris at the age of twenty-two and studied briefly in Charles Gleyre's atelier. But he was soon attracted to the work of the English Pre-Raphaelites and to the practices of more avant-garde artists, such as Edouard Manet and Edgar Degas. At times anticipating developments in the painting of these artists, Whistler exploited the inherent decorative possibilities of the flat picture plane and the compositional devices of Japanese art. This watercolor of Maud Franklin, his

108

LEFT

Maurice Brazil Prendergast,
American, 1859–1924
Reading in the Garden, c. 1892
Watercolor and pencil on paper,
8⅝ × 6½ in. (22.0 × 16.5 cm)
Signed lower right: *Prendergast*;
inscribed in margin lower left:
Reading in the Garden
Gift of Mr. and Mrs. Preston Harrison
W.938.8

109
Maxfield Parrish, American, 1870–1966
Hunt Farm (Daybreak), 1948
Oil on Masonite, 23 × 18⅞ in.
(58.6 × 47.8 cm)
Signed and dated lower right:
Maxfield Parrish / 1948;
and on reverse: *"Hunt Farm" /
Maxfield Parrish / 1948*
Presented by the artist to
Dartmouth College through the
Friends of the Library
P.950.73

model and mistress of the 1870s and 1880s, reflects both his spontaneous, lyrical handling of paint and his interest in surface pattern and linear design. The intimate interior and casual pose of the figure are analogous both in subject and treatment to the work of some of his French Impressionist contemporaries, especially Degas.   B.J.M.

108 Even in this rapidly executed watercolor dating from Maurice Prendergast's early years in Paris, we see elements of his mature Modernist style. In *Reading in the Garden* he

has already discovered a favorite subject—a fashionable lady enjoying the outdoors—and described it through the arrangement of solid patches of color. Inspired by European Post-Impressionists, particularly Paul Cézanne, Prendergast would soon take this technique to more extreme and self-conscious ends in his mosaiclike paintings and watercolors composed purely of dabs and dots of pigment.   B.J.M.

109 Through his illustrations for books, magazines, calendars, and greeting cards, Maxfield Parrish became perhaps the most familiar and popular American artist of the

first three decades of this century. Critical acclaim, however, did not come as quickly. Especially for those devoted to Modernism, his synthetic, meticulously glazed landscapes appeared too contrived, romantic, and, worst of all, too obviously commercial. Only with the more recent acceptance of the New Realists and Photorealists have Parrish's luminous, sharply focused paintings gained wider favor. *Hunt Farm*, which is believed to be an imaginary scene, was reproduced under the title *Daybreak* as a calendar illustration in 1951 and on playing cards in 1962.   B.J.M.

110
Thomas Eakins, American, 1844–1916
Portrait of John Joseph Borie III, 1896–98
Oil on canvas, 80⅜ × 42¼ in. (204.2 × 107.3 cm)
Gift of Abby Aldrich Rockefeller
P.935.1.19

110 John Joseph Borie III (1869–1925) is listed in the Philadelphia city directories of 1896 to 1899 as an architect. According to family records he worked for the firm of Cope & Stewardson, probably as a drafts-man, before moving to England permanently in 1900. He reportedly knew Thomas Eakins through the artist's close friend Samuel Murray.

By the time Eakins painted this portrait, his austere, realistic style had already met with disapproval among potential clients, and the artist was forced to limit himself to portraits of family members and friends. Although never completed, this elongated portrait shares much in common with some of Eakins's best-known works, particularly the full-length, insightful portrait of his brother-in-law Louis N. Kenton, called *The Thinker,* of 1900 (Metropolitan Museum of Art, New York).   B.J.M.

111
Frederick Childe Hassam, American, 1859–1935
Washington's Birthday—
Fifth Avenue and Twenty-third Street, 1916
Etching, second state of two,
12¾ × 7 in. (32.6 × 17.7 cm)
Inscribed, signed, and dated in plate on flag,
lower left: *New York / CH / Feb 22 1916*;
signed in pencil, lower right: *CH imp*
Gift of Mrs. Hersey Egginton in memory of her son,
Everett, Class of 1921
Pr.954.20.237

---

111 Between 1916 and 1919 the American Impressionist painter Childe Hassam created a series of paintings of Fifth Avenue in New York City called the Flag Series. In 1915, in the midst of a successful career as a painter, Hassam began to exhibit etchings and drypoints. This etching of the Flatiron Building and Fifth Avenue decked with flags for Washington's Birthday is related to the Flag Series paintings. It is one of the loveliest of the artist's etchings and one of the most impressionistic in style.

Hassam had begun his artistic career in a wood-engraving shop. Toward the end of his life, as different, more avant-garde styles of painting came into fashion, he returned to printmaking as his primary form of expression. He became a prolific etcher and lithographer and was fond of saying in his later years, "I began my career in the graphic arts, and I am ending it in the graphic arts."
J.B.

TWENTIETH-CENTURY ART

DARTMOUTH College has always collected "contemporary" art, beginning in 1793 with its commission for a portrait of trustee John Phillips (number 86). An early twentieth-century example of Dartmouth's commitment to contemporary visual expression is the 1908 painting by Frederic Remington, *Shotgun Hospitality* (number 105), which was acquired by gift in 1909. In May 1932 Dartmouth dramatized its support for the art of its own time by commissioning José Clemente Orozco's great mural cycle *The Epic of American Civilization* (number 134; see also pages 17–18). Painted in Baker Library between May 1932 and February 1934, the Dartmouth mural remains one of Orozco's most impressive works and is arguably the most important public mural in the United States.

The first major impetus to the growth of the twentieth-century collection was a gift from Abby Aldrich Rockefeller of over one hundred works of art, given in 1935. Although folk art and some nineteenth-century pieces were included, most of the works were contemporary, including paintings by George Ault, Gifford Beal, Stuart Davis, Charles Demuth (number 129), Ben Shahn (number 127), and Max Weber, and a self-portrait in bronze by Georg Kolbe.

Mrs. Rockefeller, who was a founder of the Museum of Modern Art in New York, was also the mother of Nelson A. Rockefeller, Dartmouth class of 1930. Along with his friend and colleague Wallace K. Harrison (the architect of Dartmouth's Hopkins Center), Nelson Rockefeller substantially augmented the college's collection of twentieth-century art. Their generosity, and that of Mr. and Mrs. William B. Jaffe, Mr. and Mrs. Joseph H. Hazen, and others, resulted in a significant collection of Cubist works, the centerpiece of which is Rockefeller's 1975 gift of the Pablo Picasso painting *Guitar on a Table* (number 120). Dartmouth also owns Cubist paintings by Georges Braque, Jean Metzinger, Juan Gris (number 119), and Maria Blanchard; sculpture by Jacques Lipchitz (number 116) and Henri Laurens (number 117); a substantial representation of work by Fernand Léger (see number 121); and a strong collection of Cubist prints and drawings that includes Picasso's *Vollard Suite*, given by Wallace K. Harrison in honor of Nelson Rockefeller in 1965.

Other early benefactors of the modern collection include William Preston Harrison, who gave thirty-two pictures between 1935 and 1940, and A. Conger Goodyear, who in 1940 gave ten drawings by masters such as Aristide Maillol and Henri Matisse. During the 1960s William S. Rubin was an important donor, giving paintings by Mark Rothko (number 142) and Kenneth Noland (number 143), and establishing a fund for the acquisition of modern art. In the 1960s and 1970s paintings by Fernando Botero (number 148), Alex Katz (number 147), and Jean Dubuffet (number 137), among others, and important sculpture by Sol LeWitt and Dan Flavin joined the museum's collection through the generosity of Joachim Jean Aberbach.

Thanks to the interest of Dartmouth's first gallery director, Churchill P. Lathrop, the Hood Museum is rich in work by members of the group of American

José Clemente Orozco, *The Epic of American Civilization*, detail (north wall of the east wing, Reserve Corridor, Baker Library, Dartmouth College).

East facade of Baker Memorial Library, from the steps of the Fairchild Science Center. In the foreground, Charles O. Perry's *D₂D*, bronze, 1973–75, purchase: Fairchild Fund. In the background, Beverly Pepper's *Thel*, painted steel, earth and grass, 1977, purchase: Fairchild Fund with matching funds from the National Endowment for the Arts, a Federal Agency.

painters called the Eight, especially John Sloan (see number 130), who was a cousin of Dartmouth's twelfth president, John Sloan Dickey. John Sloan was artist-in-residence at Dartmouth in 1951. Though he died later that summer, his presence continues in the form of thirty-two paintings, drawings, and prints acquired through both purchase and gift.

Dartmouth College is the home of one of this country's most venerable artist-in-residence programs, the roots of which go back to Orozco's two-year residency in the early 1930s. The ongoing presence of major artists on campus has contributed significantly to the growth of the contemporary collection. In this manner Dartmouth acquired, largely as gifts, works by Paul Sample, Lawren Harris, Friedel Dzubas, Lyman Kipp, Xavier Esqueda, George Rickey, Joseph Hirsch, Donald Judd, Richard Anuszkiewicz, Varujan Boghosian, Hannes Beckmann, Philip Grausman, Walker Evans, Jack Tworkov, Fritz Scholder, Jim Dine, Jack Youngerman, R. B. Kitaj, Ralph Steiner, Katherine Porter, Don Nice, Peter Milton, Irving Petlin,

Wolf Kahn, and Antonio Frasconi. Since the mid-1960s this program has been administered most ably by Professor Matthew Wysocki, chairman of the visual studies department.

Other highlights of the twentieth-century collection not reproduced here include paintings by Albert Marquet, Paul Klee, Reginald Marsh, George L. K. Morris, and Josef Albers; a major Fritz Glarner triptych; works by Robert Cottingham, Ron Davis, Al Held, Robert Indiana, Arman, and Ellsworth Kelly; and two early paintings by Kenneth Noland.

Dartmouth's acquisitions of the 1970s reflect the expertise of former director Jan van der Marck, whose interest in contemporary art resulted in a continuing enrichment of the collection in this area. Most of Dartmouth's modern sculpture was acquired during the van der Marck era, 1974 to 1979. As a

result, Dartmouth can claim major outdoor pieces by Mark di Suvero (number 141), Beverly Pepper, and Richard Nonas, as well as works by George Segal (number 146), Richard Serra, and Jean Tinguely (number 139). Thanks to van der Marck's efforts, Dartmouth is also the home of the George Maciunas Memorial Collection of work by artists associated with the Fluxus group, a neo-Dada movement of the late 1950s and the 1960s. This group includes work by Joseph Beuys, John Cage, Claes Oldenburg, and Nam June Paik, as well as by George Maciunas himself (number 140).

Endowment funds for acquisition are growing more rapidly for modern art than for any other part of the collection, ensuring that the Hood Museum will continue Dartmouth's tradition of strength in this area.   J.B.

112
Georges Rouault, French, 1871–1958
Head of Christ, 1913
Ceramic overglaze on porcelain,
15⅞ × 11⅞ in. (40.3 × 30.2 cm)
Signed and dated on reverse: *GR 1913*
Anonymous gift
P.979.16

113
Alfred H. Maurer, American, 1868–1932
The Clowness, 1911
Oil on canvas, 29¼ × 25⅛ in. (74.3 × 63.8 cm)
William B. and Evelyn A. Jaffe Fund
P.962.9

112 Through the Salon d'Automne and the Salon des Indépendants of 1903, Georges Rouault met André Methey, a ceramist who collaborated with many of Rouault's contemporaries and with whom he later worked on a number of ceramic pieces. From 1907 to 1913 Rouault brought the landscape and portrait themes of his paintings to plates and plaques, and nudes and prostitutes came to life on vases and platters. One of his few religious images in ceramic materials, this work is nevertheless typical of Rouault's paintings of Christ's suffering. Wounds from the crown of thorns and the tears on Christ's cheeks are painted in the same blood red; a gold-lustered border and aureole give the work an unmistakable iconlike presence. M.C.

113 Alfred H. Maurer was one of the first of the modern American artists to move to Paris. He settled there in 1897 and remained until 1914. Maurer was close to Gertrude Stein and may have seen in her home the Picasso still life *Guitar on a Table,* now in the collection of Dartmouth College (number 120). In 1907 Stein introduced Maurer to the French Fauves—painters who were attempting to convey emotion through the use of strong color and an expressive style of drawing. *The Clowness,* painted in 1911, clearly shows Fauvist influence.   J.B.

114
Auguste Herbin, French, 1882–1960
The House near the Bridge, c. 1922
Oil on canvas,
30 × 38 in. (76.2 × 96.5 cm)
Gift of Mr. and Mrs. Joseph H. Hazen
P.957.186

115
Maurice de Vlaminck, French, 1876–1958
**Saint Maffre, after the Storm
(Saint Maffre, après l'Orage),** c. 1915
Oil on canvas, 19 × 22¾ in. (48.2 × 57.8 cm)
Signed lower left: *Vlaminck*; inscribed on reverse:
10—Saint Maffre après l'Orage
Bequest of C. Morrison Fitch, Class of 1924
P.969.64.7

114 During the early period of his career, the French painter Auguste Herbin painted expressive landscapes that were strongly influenced by Cubist structure. *The House near the Bridge* is a lively painting that reveals both a coloristic talent and the compositional strength that reflects Herbin's lifelong interest in pictorial structure. Around 1926, Herbin would shift to a more abstract style that was still based on natural forms, and in 1931 he would help found the group Abstraction-Création: Art non-figuratif, intended to promote "creative" abstraction derived from geometric forms rather than from nature.

Dartmouth College owns another painting by Herbin, *Composition: The Bull*, given by Mr. and Mrs. William B. Jaffe. It was painted in 1930 and is representative of Herbin's transitional abstractions.   J.B.

115 Born in Paris of Dutch parents, Maurice de Vlaminck pursued a style of painting that combined French Modernism with the Northern landscape tradition. Vlaminck's early work was heavily influenced by that of Vincent van Gogh; however, the historic exhibitions of Paul Cézanne's oeuvre, following that artist's death in 1906, engendered a

profound change in Vlaminck's technique. His style changed from a painterly expressionism to a more classic and architectonic approach to form. *Saint Maffre, after the Storm*, although undated, is representative of the artist's mature work. Its color recalls the intense yet balanced palette of northern European landscape painting, while the oblique angling of spatial planes—the road rising on the canvas, the dynamic perspective of houses and planes of hills—attests to the importance of Cézanne in the development of Vlaminck's mature style.   P.F.

117
Henri Laurens, French, 1885–1954
Standing Female Nude (Femme nue debout), 1921
Unglazed buff terra-cotta, h. 15½ in. (39.4 cm)
Inscribed on bottom of base: *IV*
William B. and Evelyn A. Jaffe Fund
S.964.174

116
Jacques Lipchitz, American,
born Lithuania, 1891–1973
Woman Reading, 1919
Stained terra-cotta,
h. 15¼ in. (38.7 cm)
Signed on back of figure: *J. L.*;
inscribed on bottom of base: *4/7*
William B. and Evelyn A. Jaffe Fund
S.965.13

---

116 Jacques Lipchitz was part of a large group of European sculptors and painters who in the early decades of this century developed a shared Cubist vocabulary in paint, collage, clay, stone, and bronze. *Woman Reading*, a maquette for a bronze casting, is a prime example of Lipchitz's experimentation with Synthetic Cubism in three dimensions.   M.C.

117 Like Jacques Lipchitz's *Woman Reading* (number 116), Henri Laurens's *Standing Female Nude* is a representation of the female figure rationalized into a formal composition of planes, volumes, and angles. This work, and the Lipchitz to which it is closely related, are particularly appealing for their intimate scale and for the warm buff clays of which they are made.   M.C.

118
Jacques Lipchitz, American,
born Lithuania, 1891–1973
**Seated Man with a Guitar
(Study for Polychromed Bas-Relief)**, 1918
Gouache on composition board,
21⅛ × 17⅞ in. (53.6 × 45.4 cm)
Signed and dated lower left:
J. Lipchitz / 18.
Gift of Evelyn A. and William B. Jaffe,
Class of 1964H
W.959.137.6

119
Juan Gris, Spanish, 1887–1927
Mandolin and Pipe, 1925
Oil on canvas, 24 × 29 in. (61.0 × 73.6 cm)
Signed and dated lower left: *Juan Gris / 25*
Gift of Ruth and Charles Lachman
P.959.128

118 Though primarily a sculptor, Jacques Lipchitz produced throughout his career a number of drawn and painted studies for three-dimensional works. From 1916 to 1918, war-time conditions in Paris caused him to turn his energies to such studies and forced him in 1918 to move with his wife-to-be to the home of Juan and Josette Gris in southwestern France. Juan Gris was one of the masters of Synthetic Cubist painting, and this colorful work, a study for a polychromed bas-relief, reflects the interchange between the two artists that occurred in that period. M.C.

119 Juan Gris was born in Madrid in 1887; in 1906 he moved to Paris, where his association with artists of the Montmartre circle—including Pablo Picasso, Georges Braque, and Fernand Léger—drew him into the mainstream of the Cubist movement. Executed only two years before the artist's death, *Mandolin and Pipe* belongs to a series of still lifes that reveal Gris's particular brand of Cubism in that period: an adherence to the still-life subject, undulating shapes contrasted with obtuse and acute angles, and a striking sense of color. His dealer and biographer, Daniel-Henry Kahnweiler, considered the paintings of the 1920s to be "the most fruitful and beautiful of the whole of Juan Gris's work." P.F.

120
Pablo Ruiz y Picasso, Spanish, 1881–1973
Guitar on a Table, 1912
Oil, sand, and charcoal on canvas,
20⅛ × 24¼ in. (51.1 × 61.6 cm)
Gift of Nelson A. Rockefeller, Class of 1930
P.975.79

120 *Guitar on a Table*, which Pablo Picasso painted in the autumn of 1912, is a key work in the transition between the Analytic and Synthetic Cubist styles. Composed of oil, sand, and charcoal on canvas, the painting reveals the advances Picasso made in this medium that parallel the innovations of the contemporary Cubist collage technique. In September of 1912 Georges Braque introduced strips of wood-grained wallpaper into his drawing *The Fruit Dish* (private collection, France). Picasso pushed the boundary between illusion and reality even farther in a collage of the same year, *Guitar and Sheet of Music* (collection of Pedro Vallenilla Echeverrina, Caracas), by including patches of illusionistically painted wood grain in the composition. Related to the latter work, *Guitar on a Table* continues the experiment with painted patches of wood grain and the addition of sand to the oil pigment. The result is a painting that incorporates the physical textures of a collage (in the sand-textured paint), the illusion of real objects (in the trompe-l'oeil wood grain), and abstract representations of a guitar and table.   P.F.

121
Fernand Léger, French, 1881–1955
Two Profiles, No. 1, 1933
Oil on canvas,
50¾ × 38 in. (129.0 × 96.5 cm)
Signed and dated lower right:
F. LÉGER 33; inscribed on reverse:
COMPOSITION À IIV. 2 PROFILS NO. 1 F. LÉGER.33
Gift of Mr. and Mrs. Wallace K. Harrison,
Class of 1950H, in honor of
Nelson A. Rockefeller, Class of 1930
P.966.3

121 Fernand Léger's *Two Profiles, No. 1* of 1933 represents a transitional phase in the artist's work. Having matured as an artist during the Cubist period, Léger in his early work was influenced by the proto-Cubist and Cubist styles of Paul Cézanne and Pablo Picasso. In the late 1920s and early 1930s he began experimenting with the biomorphic and organic shapes of the then-popular Surrealist painters Joan Miró and Yves Tanguy. In *Two Profiles, No. 1* (*No. 2* is a horizontal version of the same composition), Léger's style has shifted from the complex color planes of his "mechanistic" Cubist style to flatter shapes silhouetted on a neutral ground. The transitional nature of this painting is also reflected in the imagery—the contrast between the rigid, geometric character of the human profiles and the organic, curvilinear shapes of the plant forms on the right. In addition to this piece, the Hood Museum owns five other paintings by Léger, a number of drawings, and twelve watercolors, including eight studies for a mural for the General Assembly Hall of the United Nations in New York.   P.F.

122 Karl Schmidt-Rottluff was one of four young Dresden architecture students who banded together in 1905 to form an avant-garde artists' association called Die Brücke—the Bridge. Along with fellow Brücke members Ernst Ludwig Kirchner, Erich Heckel, Max Pechstein, and Emil Nolde, Schmidt-Rottluff was determined to work toward a better future for mankind through art. Schmidt-Rottluff chose the name Die Brücke to symbolize the link that held the group together. Later it took on deeper significance as an expression of faith that their art would serve as a bridge to the art of the future. Members of Die Brücke were influenced by the French Fauves, by primitive art, and by German Gothic woodcuts, which served as a link with their Northern artistic heritage. These artists succeeded in creating a German version of the Expressionist style that had its origins in the work of Vincent van Gogh and Paul Gauguin. Like the Fauves, the Brücke artists were opposed to abstraction, believing that art must be rooted in natural experience; however, the German Expressionists—Schmidt-Rottluff above all—were more concerned with the expression of strong emotion than with the pictorial values that so interested the French. The medium of woodcut, with its capacity for vigorous, even harsh, expression, was a perfect vehicle for the German Expressionist style.   J.B.

122
Karl Schmidt-Rottluff, German, 1884–1976
Woman with Bowl (Frau mit Schale; Melancholy), c. 1927
Woodcut, impression 15⅜ × 19⅛ in. (39.1 × 48.5 cm)
Signed in pencil, lower right: *S. Rottluff*; inscribed on mat, lower left: *2446 / 15 Frau m. Schale*
Julia L. Whittier Fund
Pr.953.4

123
Wassily Kandinsky,
Russian, 1866–1944
Untitled, 1924
Pencil, watercolor, and
black ink on wove paper,
14¼ × 14½ in.
(36.0 × 36.7 cm)
Signed and dated lower left:
K 24; inscribed on reverse:
no. 130 [number in
Kandinsky's *Hauskatalog*] *1924*
Gift of Mr. and Mrs.
Wallace K. Harrison, Class of
1950H, in honor of Nelson A.
Rockefeller, Class of 1930
W.966.1

123 Wassily Kandinsky was born in Russia in 1866 and spent much of his career in Germany and France. In his early work Kandinsky followed the styles then popular in western Europe, Impressionism and Fauvism. These experiments with the expressive aspects of color and form fostered his move away from figurative subject matter. In 1912 Kandinsky published his famous treatise on abstraction, *Concerning the Spir-* *itual in Art*, in which he developed an analogy between abstract form and music: color, line, and shape in themselves can convey feeling, much as the sounds in music are expressive without allusion to representational subject matter. In 1922 Kandinsky joined the Bauhaus school in Weimar, where his colleagues included Paul Klee and Lyonel Feininger. This untitled watercolor, like the portfolio of prints *Die Kleinen Welt* (1922), a copy of which is in the Hood Museum collection, is characteristic of Kandinsky's style during the 1920s. More precise and geometric than the painterly works of the previous decade, this new style grew from Kandinsky's theories on form described in *Point and Line to Plane* (1926). In that treatise the artist analyzed the relationships among diagonal lines, geometric shapes, and color, thus complementing his earlier essay, *Concerning the Spiritual in Art*.   P.F.

124

Lyonel Feininger, American, 1871–1956
**Seascape with Cloudy Sky
(Marine mit bewölktem Himmel), 1922**
Blue wash and black ink on laid paper,
11⅞ × 14¼ in. (30.2 × 36.2 cm)
Signed lower left: *Feininger*;
inscribed lower center: *Marine mit / bewölktem Himmel*;
dated lower right: *Sonntag d. 4. Juni. 1922*
Gift of Daisy V. Shapiro in memory of her son,
Richard David Shapiro, Class of 1943
W.962.190

125

Lawren Stewart Harris,
Canadian, 1885–1970
Lake Superior, c. 1925
Oil on canvas, 34¼ × 40½ in.
(87.0 × 102.8 cm)
Gift of the artist in memory of his uncle,
William Kilborne Stewart, through the
Friends of Dartmouth Library
P.951.77

126

William Preston Dickinson,
American, 1891–1930
**Industrial Landscape
(The Suburbs; Modern Industry),**
c. 1918–22
Oil on canvas, 24⅛ × 19⅞ in.
(61.3 × 50.4 cm)
Inscribed on reverse: *The Suburbs*
Julia L. Whittier Fund
P.950.64

---

124 Though Lyonel Feininger was born and died in New York City, he spent more than half a century in Europe, almost entirely in Germany. As a teacher at the Bauhaus from 1919 to 1933, Feininger was associated with Paul Klee, Wassily Kandinsky, and Alexej Jawlensky, with whom he formed the Blue Four group (Die Blaue Vier) in 1926. *Seascape with Cloudy Sky* represents one of two pervasive themes in Feininger's work: the city and the sea. Its style reflects the influence of his Bauhaus colleagues' theories

in its schematic, architectonic approach to form. This example, dated 1922, is among the earliest applications of that style to a seascape subject.   P.F.

125 A pioneer member of the Canadian Group of Seven, Lawren Harris was a painter of Northern landscapes with a pronounced mystical content. He was deeply affected by Lake Superior when he first visited it in 1921, and it became one of his favorite subjects. Harris's uncle, William Kilborne Stewart, was professor of comparative literature at Dartmouth from 1919 to 1944. Partly through

this connection, Harris came to Dartmouth as artist-in-residence in 1934. He was given a number of one-man shows in the Carpenter Hall art galleries between 1936 and 1946. When Professor Stewart died in 1951, Harris gave the college this painting in his memory. The Hood Museum collection also contains a small painting of Mount Washington by Harris, a bequest of Mrs. Stewart.   J.B.

126 Born in New York City in 1891, Preston Dickinson began his training there at the Art Students League, where he studied portraiture with William Merritt Chase. Later Dickinson went to Paris, where he studied both the academic European tradition at the Académie Julian and the avant-garde styles of Paul Cézanne and the Cubists; he exhibited at the Salon des Indépendants in 1912. At the outbreak of World War I in Europe, Dickinson returned home, where he helped to shape a new artistic movement in America. *Industrial Landscape* typifies the Precisionist style Dickinson developed in New York along with painters Charles Sheeler, Joseph Stella, and Charles Demuth. Their works are characterized by a reliance on indigenous American subjects such as industrial and urban themes, precise rendering, and a mixture of realistic and abstract design. The striking coloration of this canvas, as well as the combination of painterly touches and schematic technical rendering, reveal Dickinson's personal approach to the Precisionist style.   P.F.

127
Ben Shahn, American,
born Lithuania, 1898–1969
Photographer's Window, 1939
Tempera on board, 24 × 32¼ in.
(61.0 × 81.9 cm)
Signed lower right: *Ben Shahn*
Bequest of Lawrence Richmond,
Class of 1930
P.978.165

128
Edward Hopper, American, 1882–1967
Evening Wind, 1921
Etching, 6⅞ × 8¼ in. (17.5 × 20.8 cm)
Signed in pencil, lower right: *Edward Hopper*
Julia L. Whittier Fund
Pr.956.26.5

---

127 In 1929 the painter Ben Shahn met Walker Evans, who introduced him to photography and with whom he soon shared a studio on Bethune Street in New York's Greenwich Village. Shahn's interest in using a camera to record people and scenes as sources for his paintings became a livelihood when, from 1935 to 1938, he photographed extensively throughout the South and Midwest for the Farm Security Administration. The experience produced about six thousand photographs—many of which are significant works—and it honed Shahn's profound sense of social concern. *Photographer's Win-dow* is based on a Shahn snapshot from that period (now in the Library of Congress), which is similar to Evans's well-known photo *Studio*. The snapshot shows a storefront window displaying formal portraits of well-to-do couples posed for wedding and anniversary photographs. In the painted version Shahn disrupts this image of comfortable lives untouched by the Depression by inserting subjects derived from his own photographs of the less fortunate. Here a dejected laborer interrupts the wedding views, the simple dress of a barefoot sharecropper's wife is juxtaposed with flowing bridal gowns, and the son of a rehabilitation client in Arkansas contrasts with the well-fed child decked out in bows. M.C.

128 In the decade following World War I, many American artists abandoned European-influenced avant-garde styles and shifted toward a nationalist American art characterized by naturalistic depictions of American life. Edward Hopper was one of the most important exponents of American Scene painting, although he remained a resolute individualist, never allying himself with any movement. Hopper's flat, emotionless style of painting conveyed a sense of the vacuity

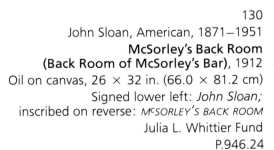

129
Charles Demuth, American, 1883–1935
Beach Study No. 3, Provincetown, 1934
Watercolor and pencil on wove paper,
8½ × 11 in. (21.4 × 27.9 cm)
Signed and dated lower left: *C. Demuth '34*
Gift of Abby Aldrich Rockefeller
W.935.1.16

130
John Sloan, American, 1871–1951
McSorley's Back Room
(Back Room of McSorley's Bar), 1912
Oil on canvas, 26 × 32 in. (66.0 × 81.2 cm)
Signed lower left: *John Sloan;*
inscribed on reverse: M^cSORLEY'S BACK ROOM
Julia L. Whittier Fund
P.946.24

of the American urban life-style. In the more intimate medium of etching, Hopper achieved a greater delicacy of feeling. This scene of a young girl distracted by a gust of wind as she climbs into bed is full of gentle mystery.   J.B.

129 Watercolor was Charles Demuth's strongest medium; in it, he created his most individualized works. Influenced in his technique by Paul Cézanne and Auguste Rodin, Demuth captures in *Beach Study No. 3* the contrast of flat color planes characteristic of Cézanne's watercolors (see number 83) and

the combination of soft washes and delicate pencil line of Rodin's figure studies. This work was produced in 1934 in Province-town, Massachusetts, where the artist spent the summer the year before his death.   P.F.

130 Between 1912 and 1930 John Sloan produced five paintings, an etching, and a number of drawings of McSorley's "Old House at Home," the bar near the Cooper Union school in New York City still popular for its ale, sharp cheddar on saltines, and light fixtures festooned with dust. "The back room was like a sacristy," wrote Sloan. "Here old John McSorley would sit greeting old

friends and philosophizing. Women were never served, indeed the dingy walls and woodwork looked as if women had set neither hand nor foot in the place." In this painting of McSorley's, from the spring of 1912 and one of two done in that year, an enveloping darkness pervades the room. A violet glow from the fireplace and the gas lamps tempers the acid light seeping through the window and barely illuminates the walls encrusted with prints, photo-graphs, and memorabilia.   M.C.

131
Lotte Jacobi, American, born Germany 1896
Portrait of Louise Nevelson, 1943
Silver print, 13⅞ × 10⅞ in. (35.3 × 27.7 cm)
Signed in pencil, lower right: *Lotte Jacobi*;
dated on reverse: *1943*
Harry S. Fisher Memorial Fund
Ph.977.196

133
Walker Evans, American, 1903–1975
Trinity Church, Cornish, New Hampshire, 1972
Silver print, 10 × 8 in. (25.4 × 20.3 cm)
Signed and dated on mat, lower right: *Walker Evans, 1972*
Gift of the Class of 1935
Ph.973.9

132
Ralph Steiner, American, born 1899
Typewriter, 1921–22
Silver print, 8⅛ × 6⅛ in. (20.5 × 15.4 cm)
Signed in pencil, lower right: *Ralph Steiner*
Harry S. Fisher Memorial Fund
Ph.975.34

131 Lotte Jacobi is a fourth-generation photographer; her great-grandfather learned the art from L. J. M. Daguerre, inventor of one of the first photographic processes. During the late 1920s and early 1930s Jacobi was among the best-known portrait photographers in Germany. She later opened a studio in New York, after fleeing Nazi Germany in 1935, and she currently lives in New Hampshire. This portrait of Louise Nevelson typifies the kind of subject that attracted Jacobi: a strong artistic personality whose own work interested her.   J.H.

132 Ralph Steiner began his photographic career when he was a student at Dartmouth College, and he subsequently achieved international prominence both as a photographer and as a filmmaker. He currently lives in Vermont, and he was artist-in-residence at Dartmouth in 1977. This image was made early in Steiner's career, when he attended the Clarence H. White School of Photography in New York. Steiner's sensitivity to the values that light etches on film yields in this photograph an elegant, almost abstract image of an otherwise commonplace object. The Hood Museum owns twenty-five additional photographs by Steiner that similarly treat "found" objects with an abstract eye. J.H.

133 Reacting to the artifice of Pictorialism in vogue in American photography of the 1920s, Walker Evans developed a straightforward, documentary style early in his celebrated career as a photographer. In this endeavor he cited the photographs that Ralph Steiner produced in the 1920s (see number 132) as an important influence. During the Depression, Evans was among a group of artists who worked as photographers for the Farm Security Administration. For several decades thereafter he wrote and photographed for major magazines, including *Fortune* from 1945 to 1965. This photograph of Trinity Church in Cornish, New Hampshire, was taken while Evans was artist-in-residence at Dartmouth College in 1972.   J.H.

a

b

c

134
José Clemente Orozco, Mexican, 1883–1949
The Epic of American Civilization, 1932–34, details
Fresco
Signed and dated on the south-wall *Machine Image* panel, lower center: *J. C. Orozco / Febrero 13, 1934*
Commissioned by Dartmouth College for the Reserve Corridor, Baker Library
P.934.13

134 Of the three great Mexican muralists from the period between the wars—José Clemente Orozco, David Alfaro Siqueiros, and Diego Rivera—the Expressionist artist Orozco was the most independent. After mural commissions at the National Preparatory School in Mexico City (1923), Pomona College in Claremont, California (1930), and the New School for Social Research in New York City (1931), all of which brought frustrations, Orozco spent happier years at Dartmouth College from 1932 to 1934. Dartmouth provided him with

an assistant professor's salary and travel funds while giving him the freedom to execute a fresco on the walls of the reserve corridor in Baker Library (see also pages 17–18 and 124). Orozco called his mural *The Epic of American Civilization*. (He also executed a preliminary panel entitled *Man Released from the Mechanistic to the Creative Life* in an adjacent corridor [b above].)

The fresco cycle consists of twenty-four compositions. In the west wing (a and d above) Orozco portrayed the golden age of the pre-Columbian culture hero Quetzalcoatl (pictured here), as he momentarily over-

comes a culture based on human sacrifice. Panels in the east wing depict the destructive tendencies brought by the Spanish conqueror Cortez, expressed through a dehumanizing machine culture. In the *Gods of the Modern World* panel of the east wing (e above), Orozco represents the perversion of learning into lifeless knowledge. The cycle concludes with a vision of the triumphant human spirit in the form of a returning

d

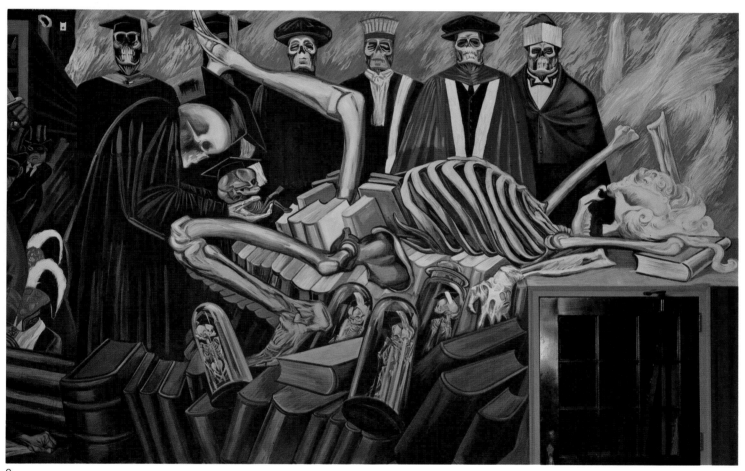

e

Christ who destroys the symbols of religious, cultural, and militaristic oppression (c above). In the center of the reading room, across from the reserve desk, is depicted a modern version of Quetzalcoatl's golden age: a society capable of collective and individual fulfillment through work and learning.

What is most striking about *The Epic of American Civilization* is Orozco's refusal to compromise his utopian message. He does not idealize the historical process, nor does he pit an innocent indigenous civilization against that of Europe, as other muralists were doing. Nor does Orozco express trust in any specific political solution. His visual epic

of the Americas is inspired by sheer indignation at the continuing degradation of the human spirit, in patterns that are hauntingly similar in ancient and modern societies. The creative potential of mankind is also celebrated, as a messianic hope that must be reimagined perpetually into the future. *The Epic of American Civilization* is Dartmouth's greatest art treasure. A source of controversy at the time it was completed, the mural is a standing testimony to the depth of the college's commitment to the principles of a liberal education.   J.B.

135
Adolph Gottlieb, American, 1903–1974
Black Enigma, 1946
Oil on canvas, 25⅛ × 32¼ in.
(63.7 × 81.6 cm)
Signed and dated lower left:
Adolph Gottlieb 46
Bequest of Lawrence Richmond,
Class of 1930
P.978.163

136
Matta (Roberto Sebastian Antonio Matta Echaurren),
Chilean, born 1912
A Pinch of Earth, 1953
Oil on canvas, 41 × 46¼ in. (104.2 × 117.5 cm)
Signed and dated on reverse: *Matta 1953*
Gift of Thomas George, Class of 1940
P.965.74

---

135 As a member of the emergent New York School of Abstract Expressionism, Adolph Gottlieb worked closely with Mark Rothko in the 1940s, developing the concept of mythic imagery in abstract painting. In 1943, three years before the creation of *Black Enigma*, he and Rothko had published a statement on their aesthetic philosophy: "There is no such thing as a good painting about nothing. We assert that the subject is crucial and only that subject matter is valid which is tragic and timeless. That is why we profess spiritual kinship with primitive and archaic art." *Black Enigma*, with its ghostly, totemic imagery on a dark ground, attests to Gottlieb's sources in Native American and African art and in the Freudian imagery of Surrealism.   P.F.

136 Born in Santiago, Chile, in 1912, Matta left in 1933 to study architecture in Paris. Influenced by the Surrealist artists he met there, he abandoned his architectural career to devote himself to painting; Matta's earliest works reflect his association with Joan Miró, Max Ernst, and André Masson. *A Pinch of Earth* typifies the artist's mature style, which integrates aspects of Surrealist painting with the Expressionism of other Latin American artists, such as David Alfaro Siqueiros. Related to another work by Matta of the same year, *To Cover the Earth with a New Dew* (Saint Louis Art Museum), this painting depicts a similar botanical fantasy: a discharging of an electromagnetic field, or the birth of new flora as the sun rises on the horizon.   P.F.

137
Jean Dubuffet, French, born 1901–1985
**Topography of a Nest of Stones
(Topographie au nid de pierres),** 1958
Oil and collage on canvas,
38½ × 60 in. (97.8 × 152.4 cm)
Signed and dated lower right: *JDubuffet 58*
Gift of Joachim Jean Aberbach, by exchange
P.975.99

138
Yves Klein, French, 1928–1962
Blue Monochrome Sponge Relief (RE24), 1960
Sponges, pebbles, dry pigment, and synthetic resin on
wood panel, 57¼ × 45⅜ × 3¾ in.
(145.4 × 115.2 × 9.5 cm)
Signed, dated, and inscribed on reverse:
1960 Yves Klein / b monochrome
Gift of Mr. and Mrs. Joseph H. Hazen
P.961.288

137 This work forms part of Jean Dubuffet's Topographies series of 1957–59. These works were made by applying sheets of variously textured materials, such as oilcloth or paper, to freshly painted surfaces and then peeling the material away. "In this way, I produced freely worked sheets that gave the impression of teeming matter, alive and sparkling, which I could use to represent a piece of ground, but which could also evoke all kinds of indeterminate textures, and even galaxies and nebulae." P.F.

138 At the age of eighteen Yves Klein began making monochromatic paintings. In an attempt to fix the "total freedom of pure and sensitive space . . . I painted monochrome surfaces," he wrote, "to see, *see* with my own eyes, what was visible of the absolute." Early experiments with a variety of colors led him ten years later to focus on an intense ultramarine blue, a color that for Klein had profound and happy associations with the sky and sea of Nice, where his family had spent summer vacations. "International Klein Blue" (I.K.B.), as he was to call it, became a dominant color in his work during

a brief but productive career. The series of sponge reliefs of which this work is a part and the related murals produced for the opera house of Gilsenkirchen, West Germany (1957–59), developed from his experimentation with sponges as a means of applying paint. For Klein the natural sponges saturated with pigment embodied his ideal of making real the deep, limitless blue of sea, sky, and space. M.C.

139
Jean Tinguely, Swiss, born 1925
Iwo Jima, 1965
Welded steel, electric motor, rollers, with wood
pedestal and foot-operated switch,
h. with base 66½ in. (168.9 cm), variable
Julia L. Whittier Fund and by exchange
S.977.22

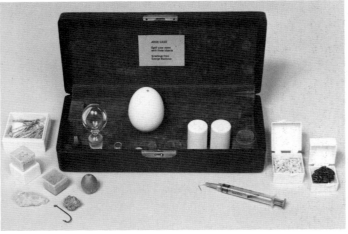

140
George Maciunas, American, born Lithuania, 1931–1978
Gift Box for John Cage: Spell Your Name with These Objects
Mixed media, box 4⅛ × 9⅜ × 2⅛ in. (10.5 × 23.8 × 5.4 cm)
Gift of John Cage
Gm.978.204.2

141
Mark di Suvero,
American, born China 1933
X-Delta, 1970
Iron, steel, and wood,
11 × 18 × 10 ft.
(3.352 × 5.486 × 3.048 m)
Gift of Mr. and Mrs. Kent Klineman,
Class of 1954
S.976.72

---

139 Jean Tinguely's fascination with motion, sound, and disorder began with a childhood pastime of constructing elaborate water-powered mechanisms that whirled frantically, hammered on tin cans at odd intervals, and gradually worked themselves to pieces. Since the mid-1940s he has devoted himself to serious play with the same "mechanics of chance," producing "metamechanicals" (automated reliefs and motorized collages of machine parts) and enormous constructions of scrap metal and dump findings that deliver chaotic, hilarious performances and end in self-destruction amid fits of dynamite,

fireworks, and flames. In *Iwo Jima* a spiral element is raised and lowered by an electric motor that whirs and shuttles back and forth endlessly. Produced just twenty years after the American invasion of Iwo Jima during World War II (it appears in a drawing of February 23, 1965), the piece recalls the fierce battle and celebrated flag-raising with the underlying irony that pervades Tinguely's work.   M.C.

140 George Maciunas was a founder and leading proponent of the Fluxus movement, "a burst of neo-Dada activities by composers,

poets, dancers, and painters in New York and Cologne at the end of the 1950s which was channeled into concert tours, festivals and publications lasting well into the 1960s." As a champion of artists' rights to live and work in former factory and business buildings in lower Manhattan, Maciunas helped to establish New York City's SoHo district. After Maciunas's death, the George Maciunas Memorial Collection of Fluxus Art was established at Dartmouth through the efforts of Jan van der Marck, then director of the Dartmouth College Museum and Galleries and a friend to many Fluxus artists and supporter of the movement.

Gift Box for John Cage is an idiosyncratic collection of benign and sinister objects packed in a used medical kit; a printed card instructs Cage to spell his name with the contents. One has the sensation on opening the box of entering fascinating but forbidden territory. Plastic boxes filled with a pine cone, bayberry, an acorn, and spices mingle with a fish hook; a blown egg, a glass bottle stopper, and a shard of amber plastic share the red-velvet-lined interior with a wad of cotton and a broken hypodermic needle. Examining the objects produces a voyeuristic anxiety like that brought on while taking stock of someone else's medicine cabinet or examining the contents of Mother's dresser drawer.   M.C.

141 Since the late 1950s Mark di Suvero, working with massive timbers, I beams, steel plates, chain, and cable, has produced bold, gestural, and infinitely graceful works that belie the mass and weight of the elements from which they are constructed. They are, in his words, ''painting in three dimensions,'' apparently effortless extensions of Abstract Expressionist vocabulary to monumental sculpture. Like many of di Suvero's works, *X-Delta* incorporates suspended sections that, when touched, transform the imposing structure into a giant plaything. The swinging of its ''bed'' produces sympathetic movement in the ''U'' of I beams hanging from the central spine; this, in turn, perpetuates the bed's motion. The viewer may bring *X-Delta* to life gently, like a hammock, or set it rocking joyously, like an amusement park thrill ride.   M.C.

142
Mark Rothko, American, 1903–1970
Orange and Lilac over Ivory, 1953
Oil on canvas, 9 ft. 9½ in. × 7 ft. 7½ in. (2.985 × 2.324 m)
Signed and dated on reverse: *Mark Rothko 1953*
Gift of William S. Rubin
P.961.123

143
Kenneth Noland, American, born 1924
Shallows, c. 1960
Oil on canvas, 9 ft. 9¾ in. × 9 ft. 10 in. (2.991 × 2.998 m)
Gift of William S. Rubin
P.961.124

142 After nearly twenty-five years of working to find the painter's equivalent of the poet's voice, Mark Rothko began in the late 1940s a series of large color-field paintings that comprise his mature work. Spare and frontal, their format is consistent: horizontal blocks or bands of color stacked two or three high nearly fill the canvas; layers of thin paint produce complex, atmospheric colors which, in Rothko's words, are an expression of "basic human emotions—tragedy, ecstasy, doom. . . . The people who weep before my pictures are having the same religious experience I had when I painted them. And if you, as you say, are moved only by their color relationships, then you miss the point." M.C.

143 An artist who began his career between the Abstract Expressionist and the Minimalist movements, Kenneth Noland reveals elements of both styles in *Shallows*. Like the Abstract Expressionist Mark Rothko, Noland used thinned oil paint to stain canvas with veils of color. Like the younger Minimalist Frank Stella, Noland approached this abstract composition non-hierarchically; that is, the forms were not placed on the canvas in correspondence to a natural scene, with elements in the lower composition suggesting a foreground space and upper sections of the canvas evoking a background. Instead, the forms were built from the center outward. The illusion of space traditionally associated with painting is thus subverted. Although undated, *Shallows* is related to a series of paintings produced between 1959 and 1961. The Hood Museum owns two additional works by Noland, *Shield* (1962) and *Advert* (1963). P.F.

144
Paul Cadmus, American, born 1904
Portrait of Francisco, 1933 and 1940
Oil on canvas, 15 × 12 in. (38.3 × 30.4 cm)
Signed upper left: *Cadmus*; inscribed on reverse of frame:
Francisco by Paul Cadmus oil, 1933 and 1940
Bequest of C. Morrison Fitch, Class of 1924
P.969.64.4

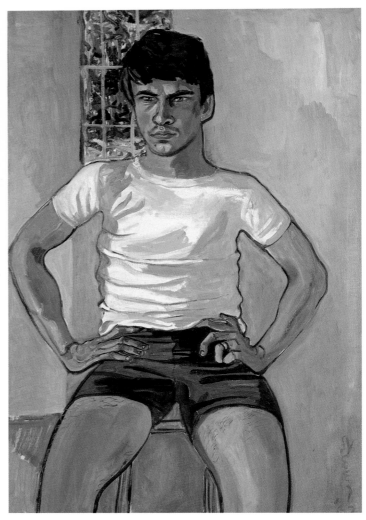

145
Alice Neel, American, 1900–1984
Portrait of Daniel Algis Alkaitis, 1967
Oil on canvas, 50 × 34 in. (127.0 × 86.4 cm)
Signed and dated lower right: *Neel '67*
Gift of Hartley S. Neel, Class of 1965AM,
in honor of Churchill P. Lathrop
P.978.155

144 Paul Cadmus is best known for his "magic realist" style (precisely rendered figures in haunting environments), for satirical paintings of Americans at home and abroad, and for his monstrous personifications of the seven deadly sins. Throughout his career, these dominant concerns have been punctuated by straightforward, sympathetic portraits of acquaintances and friends. *Portrait of Francisco* and the strong pencil drawing from which it was adapted, *Factory Worker: Francisco* (1933), are part of a group of portrayals of Spanish villagers whom Cadmus observed while living in Majorca.

Painted early in his career, *Francisco* is one of his most sensitive and beautiful portraits. M.C.

145 In the mid-1920s Alice Neel began to paint the strong, psychological portraits for which she became well known. Her "gallery" consisted of paintings of her family, friends, and neighbors and portraits of artists and business and professional people. A keen observer, Neel would first draw her subjects in thinned ultramarine paint and later add color and detail. Her portrait of Algis Alkaitis, a classmate of her son Hartley at Dartmouth,

is one of four or five works painted in his Berkeley apartment, where she and Hartley stayed during the run of her show at the Maxwell Gallery, San Francisco. The work is closely related to other portraits of her sons and their friends, in particular to a painting of Hartley done two years earlier and to a portrait of Hartley's wife, Ginny, painted in 1969. M.C.

146
George Segal, American, born 1924
Girl on a Red Wicker Couch, 1973
Plaster and wicker couch, 35 × 80 × 58 in. (88.9 × 203.2 × 147.3 cm)
Purchased with a matching grant from the National Endowment for the Arts
S.975.7

146 Dissatisfied with the limitations of painting large-scale figures, George Segal began in 1958 to explore the human form in sculptural terms. Working first with plaster and chicken wire readily available on his New Jersey farm, he constructed figures by covering wire armatures with strips of burlap dipped in plaster. A gift in 1961 of plaster-impregnated gauze bandages, newly developed at the nearby Johnson & Johnson Laboratories, revolutionized his process and launched his career as a sculptor. Segal's first figure made with this material was seated at a table in front of a window fragment, an environment that prefigured the works for which he is now well known. *Girl on a Red Wicker Couch* is reminiscent in mood of his *Lovers on a Bed II* (1970) and of a series executed in the mid-1960s of solitary, seated women brushing their hair, putting on shoes, or daydreaming in front of an open window. M.C.

147
Alex Katz, American, born 1927
Supper, 1974
Acrylic on canvas, 72 × 96¼ in. (182.8 × 244.5 cm)
Gift of Joachim Jean Aberbach
P.975.70

148
Fernando Botero, Colombian, born 1932
The Butcher Table, 1969
Oil on canvas, 71 × 61⅛ in. (180.5 × 155.2 cm)
Signed, dated, and inscribed on reverse: *Botero 69 'LA MESA DEL CARNICERO'*
Gift of Joachim Jean Aberbach
P.975.72

147 Alex Katz's portraits are arresting both for their large scale and for the flat, cool manner in which they are rendered—a painting style reminiscent at once of primitive portraits, advertising billboards, comic strips, and movie stills. In *Supper* and its companion piece in cut-out aluminum of the same year, it is as if Katz excused himself from the table and picked up a camera with a wide-angle lens. His wife, Ada (in black), and the couple with whom they are about to eat dinner seem not to notice that he—and, by exten-sion, we—observe their meal from no farther than the table's edge. Like nearly all of Katz's subjects—excepting the flowers and animals he has painted occasionally—they are members of this country's artistic and intellectual elite, engaged in familiar social rituals. Under his hand, their images become monumental icons of late-twentieth-century American life.   M.C.

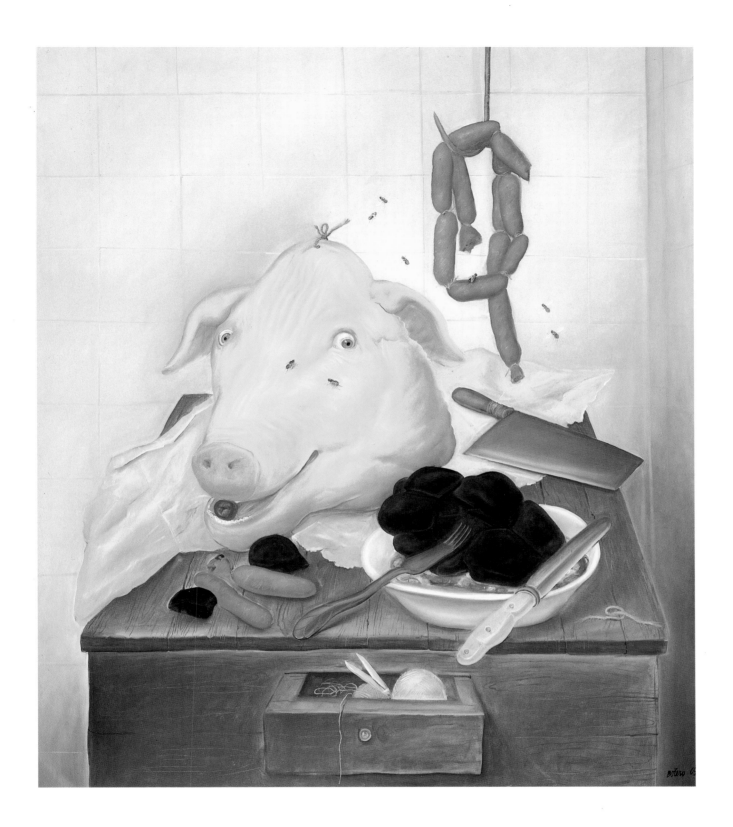

148 To enter the world of Fernando Botero's paintings is to enter a place populated by "Boteromorphs"—enormous swollen deformations of everything from Latin American dictators and figures from Old Master paintings to couples picnicking in the nude and still lifes with zeppelinlike watermelons. His canvases, at once humorously grotesque and vaguely pathetic, are described by the artist as "exaltations of life communicated by the sensuality of form." While most Boteromorphs are indifferent to, if not detached from, their circumstances, the disembodied hog's head in this work is animated by a smile and lively eyes that follow the viewer. Similar inconsistencies appear throughout the painting: the inflated fork bears stubby tines, delicate scissors and twine tucked in the drawer contrast with a plentiful bowl of globular kidneys and livers, and flies as big as the dwarf apple in the pig's mouth—or is that an olive?—buzz around the rope of plump sausages.   M.C.

149

Christo (Christo Javacheff), American, born Bulgaria 1935

Study for Running Fence 1972–76: Project for Sonoma and Marin Counties, State of California, 1976

Charcoal, pastel, printed matter, and masking tape;
two pieces: upper 15 × 96 in. (38.1 × 243.8 cm);
lower 42 × 96 in. (106.7 × 243.8 cm)

Stamped on reverse: *Christo: Running Fence 1972–76 Project for Sonoma County and Marin County, State of California. Height: 18 feet; Length 24 miles.*

Gift of Thomas G. Newman

D.977.149.1–2

149 For two weeks in September 1976, Christo's monumental ribbon of white nylon fabric snaked over hilly farmlands and through four towns in northern Marin and southern Sonoma counties in California. Emerging from the Pacific Ocean at a remote site on Bodega Bay and winding twenty-four miles east to Highway 101 near Petaluma, the *Running Fence* drew thousands of visitors, was seen on television throughout the world, and engendered a boom of cottage industries in T-shirts and tours. While the statistics of the *Running Fence* alone are impressive—four years of planning, hours of hearings with local residents, eighty-four landowners' signatures granting permission to build the project, 2,050 panels of fabric eighteen feet high and sixty-eight feet long, ninety miles of wire cable, five months of installation employing sixty-five full-time workers and 360 students at part time—it is the project's short life, as well as its monumentality, that seize the imagination. As with Christo's earlier large-scale projects—*Valley Curtain* (Rifle, Colorado, 1972) and *Wrapped Coast* (Little Bay, Australia, 1969)—and his more recent *Surrounded Islands* (Biscayne Bay, Greater Miami, Florida, 1983), all traces of the work were removed from the site after the project's completion, an aspect of Christo's work that has earned him the epithet "Manufacturer of Memories." This drawing, a study done late in the planning process, is one of the many produced by Christo and sold to raise money for the project. M.C.

150
Edward Ruscha, American, born 1937
Standard Station, Amarillo, Texas, 1963
Oil on canvas, 5 ft. 5 in. × 10 ft. 1⅝ in. (1.651 × 3.089 m)
Gift of James J. Meeker in memory of Lee English, Class of 1958
P.976.281

150 In the late 1950s and the 1960s, Los Angeles artist Edward Ruscha drove along U.S. Route 66 half a dozen times a year to visit his family in Oklahoma City. The trip inspired his first book of photographs, *Twenty Six Gasoline Stations*, published in 1963, and this painting of the Standard Station in Amarillo, Texas, produced in the same year. Like the Twentieth-Century–Fox logo in his *Large Trademark with Eight Spotlights* (1962, private collection, New York), the service station in this work is depicted with the precision of a technical rendering. Bathed in fluorescent light, the pristine structure zooms forward along the diagonal wedge of exaggerated perspective. Searchlights scan the blue-black night sky, beckoning travelers everywhere to this red-white-and-blue icon of contemporary American life.   M.C.

BIBLIOGRAPHY

ANCIENT ART

1 Assyrian Reliefs

Donald Hansen, "Ashurnazirpal's Story," *Dartmouth Alumni Magazine*, May 1952, pp. 14–17.

John B. Stearns and Donald P. Hansen, *The Assyrian Reliefs at Dartmouth* (Hanover: Dartmouth College Museum, 1953).

John B. Stearns, *Reliefs from the Palace of Ashurnasirpal II*, Archiv für Orientforschung, herausgegeben von Ernst Weidner, 15 (Graz: Selbstverlage des Herausgegebers, 1961).

Jeanny Vorys Canby, "Decorated Garments in Ashurnasirpal's Sculpture," *Iraq*, 33 (Spring 1971), pp. 31–53.

3 Cypriote Head

Douglas F. Jordan, "Four Sculptured Cypriote Heads from the Hitchcock Collection in the Dartmouth College Museum," *Dartmouth College Museum, Report for the Years 1947–1948*, p. 16.

4 Roman Sarcophagus

Adolf Michaels, *Ancient Marbles in Great Britain* (Cambridge: University Press, 1882), p. 693, no. 115.

O. Alvarez, "The Dartmouth Sarcophagus," *The Celestial Brides: A Study in Mythology and Archaeology* (Stockbridge, Mass.: Herbert Reichner, 1978), pp. 143, 274.

Jan van der Marck, *Acquisitions 1974–1978* (Hanover: Dartmouth College Museum and Galleries, 1979), p. 18.

Cornelius C. Vermeule, *Greek and Roman Sculpture in America* (Berkeley and Los Angeles: University of California Press, 1981), no. 210.

5 The Berlin Painter

J. D. Beazley, *Attic Red-Figured Vase Painters* (Oxford: The Clarendon Press, 1942), p. 214.

Dietrich von Bothmer, "A Panathenaic Prize Amphora," *Dartmouth Alumni Magazine*, June 1959, pp. 24–26.

Diana Buitron, *Attic Vases in New England Collections* (Cambridge: Fogg Art Museum, Harvard University, 1972), no. 26.

J. D. Beazley, *The Berlin Painter* (Mainz: Verlag Philipp von Zabern, 1974).

ASIAN ART

12 Hiroshige

Basil Stewart, *A Guide to Japanese Prints and Their Subject Matter* (New York: Dover, 1979), pp. 88–89.

NATIVE AMERICAN ART

13 Guanacaste Vessel

Michael J. Snarskis, "The Archaeology of Costa Rica," *Between Continents/Between Seas: Precolumbian Art of Costa Rica* (New York: Harry N. Abrams and The Detroit Institute of Arts, 1981), pp. 38, 197.

14 Morelos Standing Female Figure

David C. Grove, "The San Pablo Pantheon Mound: A Middle Preclassic Site in Morelos, Mexico," *American Antiquity*, 35 (1970), pp. 62–73.

15 Quiriguá Heads

Robert J. Sharer, "Archaeology and History at Quirigua, Guatemala," *Journal of Field Archaeology*, 5 (Spring 1978), pp. 51–70.

AFRICAN ART

34 Bamana Seated Female Figure

James Johnson Sweeney, *African Negro Art* (New York: Museum of Modern Art, 1935), pl. 5.

Paul Radin and James Johnson Sweeney, *African Folktales and Sculpture*, Bollingen Series 32 (New York: Pantheon Books, 1952), pl. 46.

39 Yoruba Staff (Eshu Elegba)

Bryce Holcombe, ed., *Yoruba Sculpture of West Africa* (New York: Alfred A. Knopf, 1982), p. 92.

40 Yoruba Staff (Orisha Oko)

William Fagg, ed., *Yoruba Beadwork* (New York: Rizzoli, 1980), pp. 46, 68.

Susan Vogel, ed., *For Spirits and Kings* (New York: The Metropolitan Museum of Art, 1981), pp. 96–98.

43 Widekum Mask

Keith Niklin, "Nigerian Skin-Covered Masks," *African Arts*, 7 (Spring 1974), pp. 8–15, 67–68.

EUROPEAN ART

53 Master of the Bambino Vispo

Jeanne van Waadenoijen, "A Proposal for Starnina: Exit the Maestro del Bambino Vispo?" *Burlington Magazine*, February 1974, pp. 82–91.

55 Schongauer

Max Lehrs, *Geschichte und kritischer Katalog des deutschen, niederländischen und französischen Kupferstichs im XV. Jahrhundert* (Vienna: Gesellschaft für vervielfältigende Kunst, 1925; reprinted Nendeln, Liechtenstein: Kraus Reprint, 1969), p. 5, no. 22.

Alan Shestack, *The Complete Engravings of Martin Schongauer* (New York: Dover Publications, 1969), no. 27.

Walter L. Strauss, ed., *The Illustrated Bartsch* (New York: Abaris Books), vol. 8, *Early German Artists*, ed. Jane C. Hutchinson (1980), no. 12 (125).

56 Dürer

Walter L. Strauss, ed., *Albrecht Dürer: Woodcuts and Woodblocks* (New York: Abaris Books, 1980), no. 50.

57 Goltzius

Walter L. Strauss, ed., *Hendrik Goltzius, 1558–1617: The Engravings and Woodcuts* (New York: Abaris Books, 1977), vol. 2, no. 283.

Walter L. Strauss, ed., *The Illustrated Bartsch* (New York: Abaris Books), vol. 3, *Netherlandish Artists: Hendrik Goltzius*, ed. Walter L. Strauss (1980), no. 142.

58 Bol

Heinrich Gerhard Franz, *Niederländische Landschaftsmalerei im Zeitalter des Manierismus* (Graz: Akademische Druck und Verlagsanstalt, 1969).

59 Palmezzano

Carlo Grigioni, *Marco Palmezzano: Pittore forlivese: nella vita, nelle opere, nell'arte* (Faenza: Fratelli Lega, 1956).

60 Attributed to Fontana

Eleanor Tufts, "Lavinia Fontana, Bolognese Humanist," *Le arti a Bologna e in Emilia dal XVI al XVII secolo*, Acts of the XXIV International Congress of the History of Art (Comité international d'histoire de l'art, 1979), vol. 4, pp. 129–34.

62 Rembrandt

Hollstein's Dutch and Flemish Etchings, Engravings and Woodcuts (Amsterdam: A. L. van Gendt), vol. 18, *Rembrandt van Rijn*, ed. Christopher White and Karel G. Boon (1969), no. B43.

64 Piranesi

Henri Focillon, *Giovanni Battista Piranesi: Essai de catalogue raisonné de son oeuvre* (Paris, 1918), no. 33.

Arthur M. Hind, *Giovanni Battista Piranesi: A Critical Study* (London: Cotswold Gallery, 1922), no. 10, i-iii.

Lawrence W. Nichols, *Piranesi at Dartmouth* (Hanover: Dartmouth College Museum and Galleries, 1976), p. 66, no. 89.

65 Saftleven

Wolfgang Schulz, *Cornelius Saftleven, 1607–1681: Leben und Werke, mit einem kritischen Katalog der Gemälde und Zeichnungen* (Berlin and New York: Walter de Gruyter, 1978), p. 249, no. 718, fig. 52.

Masters of Seventeenth-Century Dutch Genre Painting (Philadelphia Museum of Art, 1984), no. 96.

67 Goya

Tomás Harris, *Goya: Engravings and Lithographs* (Oxford: Bruno Cassirer, 1964), vol. 2, no. 269.

68 Delacroix

Alfred Robaut, *L'Oeuvre de Delacroix* (Paris, 1885; reprinted New York: DaCapo Press, 1969), p. 428, no. 1680.

69 Couture

Arthur R. Blumenthal, *Portraits at Dartmouth* (Hanover: Dartmouth College Museum and Galleries, 1978), no. 64.

Albert Boime, *Thomas Couture and the Eclectic Vision* (New Haven: Yale University Press, 1980), pp. 424–26.

71 Attributed to Brandi

Arthur R. Blumenthal, "Giacinto Brandi's *Saint Paul the Hermit and the Raven*," *Acquisitions 1974–1978* (Hanover: Dartmouth College Museum and Galleries, 1979), pp. 37–41.

72 Studio of Rubens

Svetlana Alpers, *The Decoration of the Torre de la Parada* (London and New York: Phaidon, 1971).

73 Romney

Thomas Humphrey Ward and W. Roberts, *Romney: A Biographical and Critical Essay* (London: Thomas Agnew, and New York: Charles Scribner's Sons, 1904), vol. 1, pp. 81–82; vol. 2, p. 83.

74 Beechey

Arthur R. Blumenthal, *Portraits at Dartmouth* (Hanover: Dartmouth College Museum and Galleries, 1978), no. 40.

78 Alma-Tadema

Georg Ebers, *Lorenz Alma Tadema* (New York: Gotlsberger, 1886), pp. 67–69.

Cosmo Monkhouse, *British Contemporary Artists* (New York: Charles Scribner's Sons, 1899), pp. 213–14.

C. Franklin Sayre, "Sir Lawrence Alma-Tadema's *A Roman Amateur*," *Yale University Art Gallery Bulletin*, June 1973, pp. 12–17.

Vern G. Swanson, *Alma-Tadema: The Painter of the Victorian Vision of the Ancient World* (New York: Charles Scribner's Sons, 1977), pp. 21–22, 50, 137.

83 Cézanne

Georges Rivière, *Le Maître Paul Cézanne* (Paris: H. Floury, 1923).

Lionello Venturi, *Cézanne: Son art, son oeuvre* (Paris: P. Rosenberg, 1936), vol. 1, p. 248, no. 879; vol. 2, pl. 279, no. 879.

Adrien Chappuis, *The Drawings of Paul Cézanne: A Catalogue Raisonné* (Greenwich, Conn.: New York Graphic Society, 1973).

John Rewald, *Paul Cézanne, The Watercolors: A Catalogue Raisonné* (Boston: Little, Brown and Co. and New York Graphic Society, 1983), no. 388.

84 Toulouse-Lautrec

Loÿs Delteil, *H. de Toulouse-Lautrec*, Le Peintre-graveur illustré, 11 (Paris: Loÿs Delteil, 1920), pt. 2, no. 279.

AMERICAN ART

85 and 86 Steward

Nina Fletcher Little, *Paintings by New England Provincial Artists 1775–1800* (Boston: Museum of Fine Arts, 1976), nos. 70, 71.

Thomas R. Harlow, "The Life and Trials of Joseph Steward," *Connecticut Historical Society Bulletin*, 46 (October 1981), pp. 97–127.

87 Copley

Arthur R. Blumenthal, *Portraits at Dartmouth* (Hanover: Dartmouth College Museum and Galleries, 1978), no. 27.

Arthur R. Blumenthal, "J. S. Copley's *Portrait of Governor Wentworth*," *Acquisitions 1974–1978* (Hanover: Dartmouth College Museum and Galleries, 1979).

90 Revere

Barbara McLean Ward and Gerald W. R. Ward, eds., *Silver in American Life* (New Haven: David R. Godine in association with Yale University Art Gallery and American Federation of Arts, 1979), no. 45.

91 Burt

Kathryn C. Buhler, *Massachusetts Silver in the Frank L. and Louise C. Harrington Collection* (Worcester, Mass.: Barre Publishers, 1965).

92 Dressing Table

Margaret J. Moody, *American Decorative Arts at Dartmouth* (Hanover: Dartmouth College Museum and Galleries, 1981), no. 1.

93 Attributed to Barnard

Margaret J. Moody, *American Decorative Arts at Dartmouth* (Hanover: Dartmouth College Museum and Galleries, 1981), no. 23.

Margaret J. Moody, note to "Mills Olcott and His Papers in the Dartmouth Archives," *Dartmouth College Library Bulletin*, 22 (April 1982), pp. 84–87.

95 Harding

Arthur R. Blumenthal, *Portraits at Dartmouth* (Hanover: Dartmouth College Museum and Galleries, 1978), no. 48.

96 Alexander

James Barber and Frederick Voss, *The Godlike Black Dan: A Selection of Portraits from Life in Commemoration of the Two Hundredth Anniversary of Daniel Webster* (Washington, D.C.: National Portrait Gallery, Smithsonian Institution, 1982).

Thomas Michie, "Portraits of Lawyers in the Dartmouth College Case," *Boston Bar Journal*, 27 (October 1983), pp. 13–22.

99 Sonntag

Charles C. Eldridge, *The Arcadian Landscape: Nineteenth-Century American Painters in Italy* (Lawrence, Kans.: University of Kansas Museum of Art, 1972), no. 38.

100 Vedder

Jacquelynn Baas, "*The Fisherman and the Mermaid*: A New Acquisition Reflects an Old Story," *The Quarterly: Publication of the Friends of Hopkins Center and Hood Museum of Art*, 1 (Summer 1983), pp. 22–23.

102 Gignoux

Jan Lancaster, "Régis Gignoux (1814–1882)," unpublished research paper, 1980.

103 Inness

LeRoy Ireland, *The Works of George Inness: An Illustrated Catalogue Raisonné* (Austin: University of Texas Press, 1965), pp. 387–88, no. 1482.

104 Attributed to Brooks

Frederick Fried, *Artists in Wood: American Carvers of Cigar-Store Indians, Show Figures, and Circus Wagons* (New York: Clarkson N. Potter, 1970).

109 Parrish

Coy Ludwig, *Maxfield Parrish* (New York: Watson-Guptil Publications, 1973).

111 Hassam

Royal Cortissoz, *Catalogue of the Etchings and Dry-Points of Childe Hassam* (New York and London: Charles Scribner's Sons, 1925), no. 68.

TWENTIETH-CENTURY ART

116 and 118 Lipchitz

A. M. Hammacher, *Jacques Lipchitz* (New York: Harry N. Abrams, 1975).

119 Gris

Daniel-Henry Kahnweiler, *Juan Gris: His Life and Work* (London: Lund Humphries, 1947).

120 Picasso

Christian Zervos, *Pablo Picasso* (Paris: Editions Cahiers d'Art), vol. 2, pt. 2, *Oeuvre de 1912–1917* (1942), no. 373.

Robert Rosenblum, *Cubism and Twentieth Century Art* (New York: Harry N. Abrams, 1976).

Pierre Daix, *Picasso, The Cubist Years, 1907–1916: A Catalogue Raisonné of the Paintings and Related Works* (Boston: New York Graphic Society, 1979), no. 509.

Jan van der Marck, *Acquisitions 1974–1978* (Hanover: Dartmouth College Museum and Galleries, 1979), p. 16.

121 Léger

Pierre Descargues, *Fernand Léger* (Paris: Editions Cercle d'Art, 1955), p. 103.

The Protean Century, 1870–1970 (New York: M. Knoedler, 1970), no. 34.

127 Shahn

Margaret R. Weiss, ed., *Ben Shahn, Photographer: An Album from the Thirties* (New York: DaCapo Press, 1973).

129 Demuth

Phyllis Plous, *Charles Demuth: The Mechanical Encrusted on the Living* (Santa Barbara: The Art Galleries, University of California, 1971).

130 Sloan

John Sloan: Paintings, Prints, Drawings (Hanover: Hood Museum of Art, Dartmouth College, 1981).

Grant Holcomb, "John Sloan and 'McSorley's Wonderful Saloon,'" *American Art Journal*, 15 (Spring 1983), pp. 4–20.

134 Orozco

Albert I. Dickerson, ed., *Orozco Frescoes at Dartmouth* (Hanover: Trustees of Dartmouth College, 1934).

Churchill P. Lathrop et al., *The Orozco Murals at Dartmouth College* (Hanover: Dartmouth College, Montgomery Endowment Symposium, 1980).

David Elliott et al., *¡Orozco! 1883–1949* (Oxford: Museum of Modern Art, 1980).

José Clemente Orozco 1883–1949 (Berlin: Leibniz-Gesellschaft für kulturellen Austausch, 1981).

Clemente Orozco V, *Orozco, Verdad Cronológica* (Edug and Universidad de Guadalajara, 1983).

Jacquelynn Baas, "Interpreting Orozco's *Epic*," *Dartmouth Alumni Magazine* (January–February, 1984), pp. 44–49.

135 Gottlieb

Robert Doty and Diane Waldman, *Adolph Gottlieb* (New York: Whitney Museum of American Art and Solomon R. Guggenheim Museum, 1968).

136 Matta

William Rubin, *Matta* (New York: Museum of Modern Art, 1957).

137 Dubuffet

Jean Dubuffet: Paintings (London: Arts Council of Great Britain, Tate Gallery, 1966).

Jean-Jacques Pauvert, ed., *Catalogue des travaux de Jean Dubuffet* (Paris: Max Weber, 1966), p. 14, no. 88.

Max Loreau, *Jean Dubuffet: Délits, déportements, lieux de haut jeu* (Paris: Weber Editeur, Imprimeries Réunis, 1971), pp. 272–75.

Andreas Franzke, *Dubuffet* (New York: Harry N. Abrams, 1981), pp. 111–14.

138 Klein

Pierre Restany, *Yves Klein* (New York: Harry N. Abrams, 1982).

140 Maciunas

Jan van der Marck, *Acquisitions 1974–1978* (Hanover: Dartmouth College Museum and Galleries, 1978), p. 28.

142 Rothko

Selden Rodman, *Conversations with Artists* (New York: Devin-Adair Co., 1957), p. 93, quoted in Diane Waldman, *Mark Rothko, 1903–1970: A Retrospective* (New York: Harry N. Abrams, 1978), p. 58.

143 Noland

Kenworth Moffett, *Kenneth Noland* (New York: Harry N. Abrams, 1977).

150 Ruscha

Ann Livet, ed., *The Works of Edward Ruscha* (New York: Hudson Hills Press, 1982).

Jerome Tarshis, "Ed Ruscha in Retrospect," *Portfolio*, 4 (March–April 1982), pp. 110–13.

INDEX

Page numbers in *italics* refer to illustrations

PHOTO CREDITS

Adrian Brouchard, Courtesy Photographic Records, Dartmouth College: figures 2, 7–9, 10, number 134a, c

Stuart Bratesman: page 22, number 134d

Courtesy Dartmouth College Archives: figures 5a, b, 6

eeva-inkeri: number 127

Helga Photo Studio: numbers 92, 93

Amanda S. Merullo, Williamstown Conservation Laboratory: numbers 53, 143

Jeffrey Nintzel: figure 4, pages 24, 26 bottom, 125, numbers 6, 9, 10, 15, 16, 18–20, 23, 25, 28, 36, 41, 55, 65, 85, 86, 88–91, 97, 100–102, 105, 117, 119, 130, 132, 140, 141, 144, 146, 148, 150

Jeffrey Nintzel, Courtesy Dartmouth College Archives: figure 3

Patrick J. Young: numbers 2, 3, 5, 7, 8, 11–14, 17, 21, 22, 24, 26, 27, 29–31, 33, 37, 39, 42–45, 51, 52, 56–64, 66, 68–70, 72–84, 87, 94–96, 98, 99, 103, 106–9, 111–16, 118, 121–26, 128, 131, 135, 136, 138, 145, 147